Praise for Susan Richards Shreve and *WARM SPRINGS*

"Wrenching but entirely lacking in self-pity, *Warm Springs* is both funny and revelatory, its narrator emerging as a thoroughly endearing girl poised on adolescence, who had grown up long before."

— *Boston Globe*

"One of the last generation of Americans to suffer from polio, Shreve reveals how inextricably entwined are our strengths and weaknesses, and how freedom can be as much a state of mind as of circumstance. A lovely book by a passionate and gallant human being."

— KATHRYN HARRISON, author of *The Kiss*

"Deftly weaves the historical with the personal . . . *Warm Springs* leaves powerful traces lingering in the reader's mind." — *USA Today*

"A gem of a book—an elegantly written, achingly powerful memoir of childhood illness in the terrifying era of polio. Three words best describe *Warm Springs:* riveting, honest, unforgettable."

— DAVID M. OSHINSKY, author of *Polio: An American Story*

"Extremely intense . . . The depth of human suffering here, and the bravery, are unspeakable, indecipherable. Susan Shreve has put it into extraordinary words." — *Washington Post Book World*

"What makes this memoir so extraordinary is Susan Shreve herself, whose escapades and tenderness touch and move the reader to laughter and tears and whose courage astounds us. This is a world you cannot know unless you have lived inside it. Susan Shreve has, and so will her readers." — MARY MORRIS, author of *Nothing to Declare*

"As much about a time and place as it is about the struggles of a fascinating young woman to know and accept herself." — *Chicago Tribune*

The author and her mother,
Betty Richards

With mother at Warm Springs,
circa 1951

The author (center) with Warm Springs friends and their mothers

The indoor pool at Warm Springs, used for physical therapy

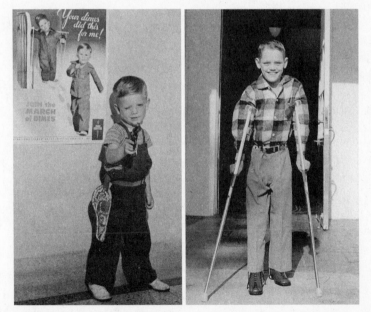

Donald Anderson, the first March of Dimes poster child, 1946

A boy tries out his new braces and crutches at Warm Springs

WARM SPRINGS

Traces of a Childhood at FDR's Polio Haven

Susan Richards Shreve

A Mariner Book
HOUGHTON MIFFLIN COMPANY
BOSTON · NEW YORK

For my only brother,
Jeff Richards

First Mariner books edition 2008
Copyright © 2007 by Susan Richards Shreve
All rights reserved

For information about permission to reproduce selections from
this book, write to Permissions, Houghton Mifflin Company,
215 Park Avenue South, New York, New York 10003.

www.houghtonmifflinbooks.com

Library of Congress Cataloging-in-Publication Data
Shreve, Susan Richards.
Warm Springs : traces of a childhood at FDR's polio
haven / Susan Richards Shreve.
p. cm.
ISBN 978-0-618-65853-4
ISBN 978-0-547-05383-7 (pbk.)
1. Shreve, Susan Richards — Health. 2. Poliomyelitis —
Patients — United States — Biography. 3. Georgia Warm
Springs Foundation. 4. Roosevelt, Franklin D. (Franklin
Delano), 1882–1945 — Homes and haunts. 5. Health
resorts — Georgia — Warm Springs. I. Title.
RC180.1. 55 2007 362.196 8350092—dc22 [B] 2006027595

Printed in the United States of America

Book design by Robert Overholtzer

VB 10 9 8 7 6 5 4 3 2 1

Photo credits: Warm Springs pool and boy on crutches,
courtesy of the Roosevelt Warm Springs Institute for
Rehabilitation. Donald Anderson, © Bettmann/Corbis.

Author's note: The incidents, characters, and places
in this book are true to my memory of them. I have
changed the names of many of the characters.

A Map to Keep

I WAS SITTING with my father on the red-flowered chintz sofa in the living room of our house in Washington, D.C., while he drew on the back of a postcard photograph of downtown Chicago along the lake. I remember the photograph because I kept the postcard folded in my wallet until a few years ago, when it disappeared.

But my father's drawing is indelibly etched in my memory.

It was the winter I was eight, and we sat side by side in front of the fireplace, late afternoon, probably a Sunday. A fire blazing, my father smoking an Old Gold cigarette, a glass of bourbon, straight up, beside him, his feet resting on the coffee table over his sleeping dog, General Beauregard, who lay under his legs.

I was anxious for no other reason except that on the rare occasions when I was alone with my father, my excitement at his unguarded attention gave me butterflies. And on this particular afternoon I must have done something to capture this attention or to reveal a failure of character sufficient to stir his parental instincts, which were not easily stirred.

"This dot is you, Susan Lynn Richards," he began with his inclination to exalt our lives. "Age eight and a half, citizen of the United States of America."

He indicated a tiny dot he'd made in the middle of the postcard.

"And this dot is you in the circle which represents your family," he went on. "Your mother and me and Jeffrey and General Beauregard and Grandma Richards and the visitors who sometimes spend the night."

Visitors often spent the night at our house, and they might or might not be related to us. Sometimes they were people my father took in simply because it was in him to do that, and I didn't want to consider them part of my family because they were usually drunk, which I told him.

"When these visitors are in our home, they're part of our family," he said, drawing a slightly larger circle. "And this is your neighborhood, called Cleveland Park, in Washington, D.C." He drew a circle for the city of Washington and then one for the country and another for the continent and then the hemisphere and finally the world.

The tiny dot seemed smaller and less central as the circles grew in size.

"What about the stars?" I asked. "Aren't you doing the universe?"

"I'm sticking to the places where we know that human beings live," he said, "and we don't know about the stars."

Then he used a blue pencil to indicate the oceans, and a green one for the land, and handed the postcard to me.

"Get it?" he asked.

"I do," I said.

But I didn't get it at all, beyond an understanding that the diminishing dot was me.

I kept the picture because my father had drawn it for me.

When I decided to write about the two years, between the ages of eleven and thirteen, when I had lived at the Warm Springs Polio Foundation, thinking how to frame the book, how to imagine a structure that would allow for my memoir to be a detail in an expanding landscape of a person and a place and a certain history, I thought about my father's drawing.

This small story of my two years at Warm Springs is told against the larger story of my family, of a time and place, of racism and religion, of the first major public health success in the United States, and of President Franklin Roosevelt, who created the place called Warm Springs, which for a while a lot of us called home.

I

....

Go In and
Out the Window

Traces

I'M SITTING WITH my legs straight out on an examining table at the Georgia Warm Springs Polio Foundation, where I have just arrived. Four doctors lean over my legs, their elbows on the table, talking back and forth. The doctors are looking for traces.

Traces are little whispers of life in muscles destroyed by the polio virus. They promise the possibility of a new future. My part in this examination, not the first in my life with polio, is to concentrate with all my might on each muscle, one at a time, in the hope that with my undivided attention, there will be a shiver of response and the doctors will rise up, smiling, and announce that the audition has been a success and there is reason for hope.

Muscle to muscle, trace to trace, I am looking for a sign of possibility.

At Warm Springs, traces is the word for hope.

When I think of the word "traces" now, it is as a footprint or a shadow or a verb, like "unearth" or "expose" or "reveal."

I've been looking for traces in my childhood that will bring the years I spent in Warm Springs into some kind of focus. In its intention, the process is very much the same as it was when I lived there and turned my attention to discovering what remained.

Warm Springs, 1952

ON THE MORNING Joey Buckley got his wheelchair back, got to leave his bed and move about the hospital grounds alone, I had been up at dawn, before the Georgia sun turned the soft air yellow as butter. I lived in the eighth bed in a sixteen-bed ward of girls at the Warm Springs Polio Foundation and had been living there, off and mostly on, since I was eleven years old. That morning, at the beginning of April, I was wide awake with plans to slip out of the room without any of the fifteen other girls knowing I was gone until they woke to the rancid smell of grits and eggs to see my empty bed carefully made.

I was wearing blue jeans, cut up the seam so they'd fit around my leg cast, a starchy white shirt with the collar up, a red bandanna tied around my neck like Dale Evans, my hair shoulder length, in a side part, the June Allyson bangs swept up in a floppy red grosgrain bow. A cowgirl without the hat and horse, a look I cultivated, boy enough to be in any company.

I wheeled past Avie Crider on the first bed, lying on her left side, her right leg hanging in traction above her hip, a kidney-shaped throw-up pan by her cheek. She'd come out of surgery the day before, screaming all night, but we were used to that in one another and could sleep through noises of pain and sadness, or talk through them, about movies and boyfriends and sex and God, back and forth across the beds. Never pain and sadness.

I shut the door. The Girls' Ward (called Ward 8 by the staff), on the second floor of Second Medical, was at one end of a long hall, and the Boys' Ward was at the other end. The long corridor, with the nurses' station between the wards, was empty at dawn, too early for the smell of breakfast, for the morning nursing staff to click up and down the corridors with trays of thermometers and medicines, even for the bedpans, which were my responsibility.

I wanted to go straight to the Boys' Ward, where Joey Buckley might be waiting for me, but it was too early for that also, too early for mail, which was my other job, or for orderlies to take the surgery patients down to the first-floor pre-op waiting room, or for the domestic staff to begin mopping the linoleum for a new day. Too early for anything but the Babies' Ward (officially called the Children's Ward), where I went every afternoon to take the babies in my lap for a wheelchair spin around the walkways, pretending they were mine for keeps, these orphan babies whose parents were off in their own houses in other towns, like my parents three hundred long miles away in Washington. These babies couldn't do without me.

But this morning, days away from thirteen, a girl of high temperament and little patience, I was burning with anticipation. I wanted to go as fast as a girl could go, a winged runner with hair on fire, hanging over the side of an open cockpit, a high wind blowing my clothes off.

I passed Miss Riley, the red-haired head nurse, her long, freckled legs stretched straight out from the chair where she was sleeping, her head thrown back against the wall, her mouth hanging open. My wheelchair was standard issue, made of wood with yellowed wicker on the seat and back, and it was squeaky so I pushed it softly by Miss Riley's office, down the corridor to the elevator, hoping not to get caught before I carried out my plan.

When the elevator doors opened onto the first floor, Dr. Iler was rushing out of the Babies' Ward, and I waved, but he looked right at me without registering who I was or wondering, as he ought to have, what I was doing up and dressed at dawn. Running away? That's what he would have thought if he'd seen me through his own preoccupations. On bad days, running away was what we talked about doing, as if we had legs for running or anywhere to go, stuck in the Georgia countryside, prisoners of our own limitations.

"Suzie Richards." Dr. Iler suddenly stopped and turned around, as if my presence had come to him in memory after he had seen me in person. "What are you doing up at the crack of dawn?"

"I couldn't sleep," I said.

"Well, be careful," he said, and I thought to say "Of what?" out here in the middle of mainly nowhere with doctors and nurses and priests and orderlies, no danger here except the invisible one of my own secret desires. But what did I know then about fear of what was inside myself?

"I will be careful," I said, and he was gone.

Outside the front door, the air was New England chilly, fresh with the beginning of spring, and I wheeled my chair through the big door, down the ramp onto the sidewalk, thinking of Joey Buckley's brown eyes, deep and dark as winter ponds.

The buildings of the Warm Springs Polio Foundation had a kind of fading beauty. It had been a late-nineteenth-century spa, rebuilt, after Roosevelt purchased the old Meriwether Inn and grounds, with low white buildings in wings around a grassy courtyard with walkways, some covered like porticoes. I thought of myself as living in a hotel. I was grown-up and beautiful and walking without the aid of crutches or braces, walking in high heels, and I had come to this hotel on a holiday to find the man of my dreams.

I wheeled over to the wing where the Boys' Ward was located, stopping just below it so Joey Buckley, if he happened to be looking out the window beside his bed, would see me there.

Behind me, the door to the main building opened and shut, and I kept my back to whoever was coming out, hoping to pass unobserved, but the invader of my private romance was Father James, another recipient of my unguarded affection, and he had seen me. I could feel him headed in my direction.

"Mary," he said, coming up behind me, out of breath.

He called me Mary because I had told him my middle name

was Mary and I was called by that name at home, although my middle name was really Lynn. But neither Susan nor Lynn seemed right for a Quaker girl converting to Catholicism, as I had been in the process of doing with Father James, wishing to fill the long empty hours with something commensurate with my desire and because I loved him and believed he would like me better with a name like Mary.

Much of my free time at Warm Springs was spent figuring out the best way to be liked by the people I wanted to like me. Not everyone. Only the ones who judged me bad for reasons I could never understand, neither the reasons nor the meaning of bad. And the ones I adored, since I was at an age and had an inclination to love without reservation.

"What are you doing up so early?" Father James gave my wheelchair a gentle push.

"I couldn't sleep," I said. "What about you?"

He hesitated, and I could tell even before he spoke that he was inventing some excuse for being in the hospital when he normally would be getting ready to serve at the 6 A.M. Mass, generally attended by the staff at Warm Springs either on their way to work or on their way home.

"Did something happen to one of the babies?" I asked. "I saw Dr. Iler."

"Dr. Iler was in the Babies' Ward," he said.

"Were you there for a sick baby?" I asked.

And I suddenly remembered our recent conversation in catechism class about last rites. I had been fascinated and repelled by the idea of a priest, a man in a stiff white collar and black robe but still a man, ridding the dying of leftover sins so that, *fresh as a daisy*, as my mother would say, the dead could pass into heaven. I loved the Roman Catholic Church, with the body and blood of Jesus popped into our mouths and incense burning and bells and chanting in Latin. But passing into heaven held no appeal at all.

"Were you in the Babies' Ward doing last rites?" I asked, my mind running through the cribs of babies, Eliza Jane, little Maria, Tommy Boy, Rosie, Sue Sue, Violet Blue, Johnny Go-Go, all those babies of mine with the nicknames I had given them.

"Don't go into the Babies' Ward today, Mary."

"Can you tell me which baby?" I asked.

He tousled my hair.

"Not just now," he said, and I watched him walk away in his black cassock, his muddy shoes showing below the skirt, his long thinning hair flying above his head in threads.

Halfway across the courtyard, he turned and, with his cassock blowing behind him, walked back toward me.

"Mary," he said, kneeling so we were face to face. "I know you're thinking you'll go to the Babies' Ward as soon as I'm out of sight, but you can't. This was not a patient you knew."

Instinctively I didn't believe him.

I watched until he was out of sight and then I crossed the courtyard on a diagonal toward the movie theater — not an actual movie theater but a large room where current Hollywood films were shown to the patients, mostly children, either sitting in wheelchairs or lying on stretchers in body casts, everyone in the hospital who could breathe without an iron lung, in rows of white sheets.

The next afternoon, a Saturday, I would be going with Joey Buckley to see *High Noon* — that was the description of my Saturday I would tell my parents during our Sunday telephone call, always just after noon, a ritual of longing and dread.

"I went to see *High Noon* with Joey Buckley," I'd say. "We do everything together lately."

I knew it would please them to hear that I had a best and steady friend, a Joey Buckley whom they'd met but didn't know, filling the gap their absence had left. It would please them to think of me doing the things that normal children in the sixth grade did, like going to movies.

It wasn't necessarily true about Joey Buckley. I'd usually be in line with all the girls from the Girls' Ward in wheelchairs, and we'd follow the stretchers moved by push boys, and behind would be the line of wheelchairs from the Boys' Ward, and then the grown-ups who had the freedom to move, if they could move, out of the lineup. When I saw Joey, he would be in a line of wheelchairs behind me, several boys away.

I saved stories for my parents to make them happy, to soften their sadness over not being with me, which I knew they wished they could be, which I wanted to believe they wished they could be. And the stories had some truth, along with the addition of a happy ending. I added the happy ending perhaps by nature, perhaps in my own defense. A child can cover a multitude of sadness simply by inventing happiness, can escape the kind of sympathy that smothers her spirit, and save her fledgling self in its slow and lonely process of definition.

All week I'd think of the conversation I'd have with my parents the following Sunday after church, collecting imagined victories, social engagements, popularity, good behavior, although I had not told them I was going to Mass every Sunday or how little I missed the long silence of Quaker Meeting, only that noon was the best time for them to call.

I had it in mind to draw the picture of a busy twelve-year-old girl living an ordinary life in a hospital at which children got better and better and never died. I would tell them of crushes and best friends and compliments from doctors on my progress and athleticism, from nurses on my good citizenship and work on behalf of others. I was, in short, deliriously happy at Warm Springs, as they desperately hoped I would be, and grateful for the opportunity to get better for free, costing my parents almost nothing, as a result of President Roosevelt's March of Dimes, money collected in a highly successful campaign held every year on the anniversary of the president's birth, which supported, among other things, the treatment of children at Warm Springs.

Stopped in my wheelchair in a corner of the courtyard, thinking of the dead baby, some dead baby passing sinless into heaven, substantial or insubstantial — I just didn't think it was possible or desirable, and the thought of it, dying and going to heaven, was unacceptable. I wanted to call my mother, my darling mother, and tell her, "A baby died today in the Babies' Ward," and hear her soft, magical voice pressed to the receiver, saying my name. "Susan." But of course I would never tell my parents that a baby had died. It would frighten them, so far away from me, so vulnerable to my fate.

My plan for the day, after Joey Buckley got his wheelchair, was to go with him to the candy shop, where we got to go sometimes twice a week, always on Fridays, and this was a Friday. We'd get cheese crunchies and Grapette and sit in the sun behind the buildings, where no one would expect to see two patients sunning. I'd buy him bubblegum with baseball cards as a present for getting over surgery and we'd talk. I was an excellent listener.

And when we'd finished our snacks and I had hold of little pieces of Joey Buckley's life, we'd race our wheelchairs down the steep paved hill where on Saturday afternoons the stretchers and wheelchairs wound their way down the path between the buildings from the courtyard to the movie theater.

I wheeled across the courtyard to the top of the paved hill and looked down. I was good with a wheelchair. I could push the chair up to a high speed, take hold of the right wheel with a strong grip, and make a 180-degree spin so that my body, like a keeling racing sailboat, was nearly parallel to the sidewalk. I could wheel up that hill without stopping, without slipping backward, my hands like little vises on the wheels, the bone showing through the skin. I wanted to move as fast as the chair would go — crouch my body down low so my head was just over my knees stretched out in front of me. I stopped at the top of the hill on level ground just before the bend, but if I were to move inches into the downgrade, the chair would be off on its wild ride to the bottom of the hill and I'd be holding on for dear life. That's how I saw myself, and imagining the speed, imagining Joey Buckley flying beside me, our hands on the wheels, ready to stop on a dime, I decided we'd do just that — we'd race down the hill this morning, early, before too many people were sitting around the courtyard on such a fine day. First, before doing anything else, we'd race to the bottom and secure our friendship like surviving warriors. We'd make it to the bottom and fall into each other's arms.

I had arrived at Warm Springs in the late summer of 1950, on the same day that Joey Buckley arrived in his leather and aluminum chair, both legs crippled, in long leg braces, a motherless boy from a small town in Alabama. I was alert to his presence, greeting every new face as a possibility, and I liked the way he looked with his square face and wide-set brown eyes. In the waiting room as we checked into the hospital, his father sat next to my mother and I remember the image of him exactly: olive skin, broad face, and long shiny hair, his head held in his big hands as if it had cut loose from his body.

"Joey would have been an athlete. He would have been a great athlete, this boy," his father told my parents. "He would've played football at Alabama, and now what?"

"Now I'm going to be fixed, Papa," Joey said. "You too?" he asked me.

It was still early morning, breakfast trays collected in the wards, meds distributed, plans in place for the rest of the day. Joey and I were parked at the top of the steep hill, looking down.

"It's a long way to the bottom," he said.

I was checking Joey's casts, sticking out in front of him propped on pillows, blood seeping through the plaster at the top of both of the casts.

"The blood's from my stabilization incision," he said, conscious that I was looking at it. "You bled too, right?"

"Right," I said, a shadow of doubt, a cloud floating across my sun. "But I had only one stabilization and you had two, so that's a lot of blood."

"It'll dry up," he said. "So why are we doing this?"

"For fun," I said. "Just for fun, don't you think?"

"Yes, for fun," he said. He was smiling and his eyes lit up and I knew we were ready to push off.

"Hand in hand?" I called to him.

"I can't push if we're holding hands," he said.

And lined up side by side, we gave a huge push on the metal ring on the wheels of our chairs and we were off down the hill, faster and faster, and I think I was squealing with excitement and so was Joey and maybe he called out "How do we stop?" but maybe he didn't. We were going so fast, so much faster than I even imagined in my dreams of this adventure, I felt that I was losing control, the bottom of the hill rising to meet us as we sailed down side by side, and I grabbed the right wheel to stop the momentum, grabbed it with all my might so the chair would turn 180 degrees and stop there at the bottom. And as I did, sensing that the chair would stop, that I had taken control in the nick of time, I saw Joey fly into the air just ahead, out of his wheelchair, the chair tipped on its side and Joey gliding above me, his arms flailing, his heavy white casts pulling him down, down, down to the cement walk and then the heavy thud of the casts hitting the ground or the thud of his head and silence.

A Brief History of
Warm Springs Polio Hospital

October 1924–August 1950

WARM SPRINGS was a village, is still a village, of fewer than a thousand permanent residents, located eighty miles southwest of Atlanta. It was a stop on the Columbus, Georgia, milk train in the twenties, approached then by a narrow, bumpy dirt road. At the turn of the century it had been a popular spa resort where vacationers came to escape the sultry southern summers and the rising industrial pollution in the cities, to take the warm mineral waters at the pool of the Meriwether Inn. But by 1924, when Franklin Roosevelt arrived at the Warm Springs railway station with Eleanor Roosevelt and his secretary, Missy Le Hand, the Meriwether Inn, co-owned by a friend of Roosevelt's, was a rundown shamble of Victorian gingerbread architecture, and the simple cottages around the inn — in one of which Roosevelt set up housekeeping on the first of his many visits — had neither electricity nor plumbing.

Roosevelt had come for the mineral waters.

In late summer of 1921, as outbreaks of poliomyelitis escalated to epidemic proportions in the United States, Roosevelt, on holiday with his family on Campobello Island, off the coast of northern Maine, came down with the paralytic strain of the polio virus and was gradually paralyzed below the neck.

He was thirty-nine years old, with a promising political career, a professional marriage, and five young children — and he'd been having a long-running love affair with Lucy Mercer, Eleanor's personal secretary. At the time of his illness, he had served four years in the New York State Senate as a Democrat in a Republican district, had been appointed by Woodrow Wilson as assistant secretary of the navy in 1914, and in 1920 had been nominated as his party's vice presidential candidate, to run in an unsuccessful campaign with James Cox.

In newspaper accounts from those years, he is described as a skillful speaker, with the jovial charm and easy confidence of his protected class, but neither reflective nor intellectual, and not particularly serious. As one reporter summarized it, Franklin Roosevelt was an affable, decent, moral man, a leader by nature, but finally a lightweight unacquainted with grief.

His initial reaction to his illness was stoic denial. He maintained absolute confidence that he would walk again, even when he had been told he would not. Eleanor Roosevelt said, "There were certain things he never talked about — he would just shut up." "Certain things" included death and disability. He never, according to Eleanor, said he could not walk, insisting on good cheer without complaints even during the most painful months following the onset of polio. This brave invention lasted throughout his life and political career, in which his crippled condition was concealed by the construct of a "splendid deception" — his wheelchair seldom visible in photographs, and his habit of holding on to someone's arm instead of using crutches when he stood. But he couldn't walk, and when he stood, he was supported by braces from his ankles to the top of his thighs, locked at the knees so he wouldn't topple. As recently as the late 1990s, there was an ongoing debate, reflecting his own insistence on appearances, on whether or not to have the FDR memorial in Washington, D.C., include his wheelchair. Things were finally resolved in favor of the wheelchair.

Polio has had many names, among them infantile paralysis, since young children, with immune systems not yet fully developed, were the most frequent victims. Poliomyelitis is the scientific term, from the Greek *polios*, meaning gray, and *myelos*, meaning core — so named because the scarred area of the body in a case of polio was the cable of gray matter running down the center of the spinal column. By the twentieth century, when outbreaks of polio became epidemic in Europe and North America, the disease had been around for many centuries, recorded in images of crippled children with characteristic bone-thin legs and dropped feet, and found even in Egyptian mummies. But as a widespread public health issue, the prevalence of the disease increased with sanitation efforts following industrialization. Most commonly affected were the unprotected privileged, who were so seldom exposed to crowded conditions that their immune systems were undefended against the virus.

I grew up believing, as most people did, that polio was a disease of the poor, who played in public places and lived in overcrowded conditions. It was well known that the virus was passed through feces, and some of the shame associated with the illness had to do with class.

But it was a false premise. The disease itself, and then the shame of the disease, present in every culture and epidemic in the puritanical upper classes, suggested moral laxity and a failure of will. Will, in this case associated with an idea of perfection, ought to protect a person from illness. A failure of the body reflected a weakness of character, or so it was seen.

By the middle of the twentieth century, three separate polio viruses had been identified by scientists. The most common of these has the symptoms of influenza, with high fever and muscle aches, and disappears after a couple of weeks with no residual damage. Many people, including children, had this strain without ever knowing they'd contracted anything more serious than the flu. The least frequent and most damaging of the viruses is that of bulbar polio, which attacks the medulla oblongata, the part of the brain that controls autonomic functions such as breathing and relays signals between the brain and the spinal cord. We are most familiar with this crippling strain of the virus, which affects the limbs — usually, as in the case of Roosevelt, the legs.

During the active life of the virus, the limbs are so painful that a patient cannot bear to be touched, even by sheets.

Roosevelt was left crippled from the waist down. For the next seven years he refused to accept permanent paralysis, dedicating himself full time to his own rehabilitation, living at his mother's house in Hyde Park, sometimes in Florida, eventually in Warm Springs, following a spartan regime of exercises, determined to recover the use of his gradually atrophying legs.

Eleanor Roosevelt and FDR's political adviser Louis Howe, who moved into the Roosevelt home and remained there throughout the president's life, continued Roosevelt's political career from New York without him, concealing the severity of his handicap from the public in an atmosphere, still lingering, in which physical disability was an indication of a weakness of character.

In October 1924, when Roosevelt arrived in the farm community of Warm Springs, located on high ground in the Pine Mountains of Georgia, he set up housekeeping in one of the primitive cottages. Eleanor stayed briefly, uncomfortable in a rural setting in which chickens were bought live and killed for dinner, and disturbed by the treatment of blacks and the general narrow thinking of white southerners. But Franklin Roosevelt had found a new home.

He had come on the advice of his friend George Carter Peabody, the co-owner of the Meriwether Inn with a man named Tom Loyless. Peabody had told Roosevelt of the success of a young polio — we were referred to as "polios" — who had gradually learned to walk again after swimming in the mineral waters of Warm Springs.

Roosevelt planned to walk again. Long after he was told by orthopedic doctors that his legs were damaged beyond repair, even after he realized that fact himself, he still believed it could be possible for him to change the prognosis.

When I was at Warm Springs we had a "fight song" — probably there had always been fight songs. Certainly the spirit of them, if not the songs themselves, originated with Roosevelt. Our fifties song was sung to "Music! Music! Music!" ("Put another nickel in / In the nickelodeon"), and it went like this:

> Put another muscle in
> Where the quadriceps have been
> 'Cause we know we'll never win
> With traces, traces, traces.
>
> What's the use of stretch and strain
> What's the good of pull and pain
> When our muscle tests remain
> Just traces, traces, traces.
>
> They push our torso
> And make it more so
> When we try to make a muscle go
> It's substitution, no, no, no.
>
> So even though our hopes have soared
> Higher than our muscles scored
> Just the same we thank the Lord
> For traces, traces, traces.

Roosevelt had traces in his withering legs — whispers of muscle response, promising, maybe only teasing, that hard work and determination and constancy might resurrect the life in muscle. He had reason for optimism.

On Roosevelt's first morning at Warm Springs, he met Louis Joseph, the young man who had learned to walk after swimming in the warm mineral waters. Together they devised a regime of exercises for Roosevelt, which he would follow and teach to other polios over the next twenty-one years of his life as a visitor or resident of Warm Springs.

The highly mineralized springs rise from the Pine Mountains and flow at the rate of 1,800 gallons a minute, remaining at a temperature of 88 degrees. The waters, as it turned out, were not specifically curative for any of us who bathed in them, but they had a remarkable buoyancy, which countered the pull of gravity and gave the handicapped bathers a sense of moving with an ease impossible on dry land.

For the first time, Roosevelt was actually able to walk on his own in the water without falling. But of course walking was an illusion, a result of the buoyant water and not of traces that could be coached to life.

Shortly after Roosevelt's arrival in Warm Springs, the *Atlanta Journal* sent a reporter to write a story about his visit, which appeared in late October in the *Journal*'s Sunday magazine under the title "Franklin D. Roosevelt Will Swim to Health." The article was reprinted across the country and read by many polios. Roosevelt had already spent hours with Tom Loyless talking about revitalizing the Meriwether Inn and developing a convalescent rehabilitation center for the victims of infantile paralysis, who would live among the able-bodied guests of the old inn.

After the *Atlanta Journal* article appeared, letters began to pour in from polios all over the country, and some polios were desperate enough to arrive at Warm Springs without invitation or notice. The response astonished Loyless and Roosevelt. The inn, still hoping to attract its usual visitors, was not designed for wheelchairs. There were many steps and narrow doorways; the cottages had no bathrooms. There was no therapeutic equipment, and no research studies had been conducted, as would be required today. No medical clearance was given, no standards were set, no physicians were in attendance.

One day, so the story is told, Roosevelt and Tom Loyless and some neighbors were sitting on the porch of the inn when a messenger came up the hill to say that two people had arrived by train who couldn't walk, and what should be done with them? The decision was made to put them up in the village and to fix up one of the wrecks of a cottage for them. By the time that cottage was put in order for the two new arrivals, eight more had come. That was the fall of 1924. By the following summer, there were more than twenty-five patients.

That summer of 1925, with Loyless too ill with cancer to work, Roosevelt took over the operation of what would become the Georgia Warm Springs Polio Foundation. He had ramps built into the inn, cottages repaired, and he personally designed a water table, which sits a foot beneath the surface of the water and is still used for hydrotherapy. He devised exercises and treatment programs, drew up muscle charts, worked with the patients on their exercises.

He gave the polios what he himself had found, a home of their own with people like themselves, like him, a kind of substitute family in a place where they were expected to work hard and laugh hard and to reach for their highest expectation of themselves. They called him "Doctor Roosevelt," and he called himself Doctor too, saying in a speech at Warm Springs after he became president of the United States that he hoped, once his work in Washington was done, he would be welcomed back into the medical establishment at the foundation. He became a consulting architect and landscape engineer, designing a new water system, a sewage plan, a fishing pond, and a club that would have a dance hall and a tea room, indoor and outdoor sports.

Roosevelt was a "holistic physician" before that concept became a term of art, and established his beliefs as practice at Warm Springs. Patients came and stayed because they had found a home. Fred Botts, the business manager when I was there, had been among the first patients, back in the twenties, some of whom traveled to Warm Springs by hiding out in freight cars, near death from heat and starvation by the time they arrived. (I know that they rode the cars but not how they got on them in the first place.)

When I visited in 2006, new pillars in the hospital's courtyard colonnade had replaced the original ones, modeled by Roosevelt after Thomas Jefferson's design for the University of Virginia. The new pillars tell a story of gratitude, donated by patients who stayed at Warm Springs for many years, met their wives or husbands, made a life there.

In the spring of 1926, against the strong advice of his wife, his mother, and his law partner Basil O'Connor, Franklin Roosevelt bought Warm Springs, committing two thirds of his personal fortune to the purchase.

He brought in an orthopedic surgeon to be in charge of the medical program and a physical therapist who had worked with polio since the 1916 epidemic in New York, and he set about seeking the endorsement of the American Orthopedic Association. After a study of twenty-three patients in treatment, the association concluded that there was marked improvement in each of the cases, and endorsed Warm Springs as a hydrotherapeutic center.

In 1927, Roosevelt and O'Connor established the Georgia Warm Springs Polio Foundation (the name was changed to the National Foundation for Infantile Paralysis after Roosevelt was elected president) as a permanent nonprofit institution to provide funds for polio research, particularly to the laboratory of Jonas Salk, through the March of Dimes and the President's Birthday Balls, held as fund-raising events all over the country on Roosevelt's birthday. In these ways, the foundation became the vital source of funding for the first major public health triumph in the United States. That same year, the paying guests at the Meriwether Inn, less and less happy to be sharing their vacation with the polios, were sent away and a master plan for construction of the hospital was designed.

At the heart of Warm Springs was Roosevelt's deep belief that the rehabilitation of the polios was a social problem with medical considerations rather than a medical problem first. The hospital became a community of the handicapped, living and working together to repair their lives in a beautiful setting with bright rooms and good food. It was envisioned as a place where fun was central to daily life, where people could sing and dance and talk and fall in love.

Roosevelt had gone to Warm Springs to recover. He imagined that he would leave the mineral waters walking unattended, without crutches or braces. Sometime between 1927 and his first presidential race, he realized that he would never walk again. But he must have known that what he had accomplished at Warm Springs was not just the creation of a rehabilitation center but a revolutionary concept of treatment.

In September 1937, the first year of his second term as president, Roosevelt announced the nonpartisan National Foundation for Infantile Paralysis, changing the name of the Georgia Warm Springs Polio Foundation to expand the mission and separate the foundation from his Democratic presidency. The newly named foundation had the goal of leading and unifying the fight against every phase of polio. By 1945, the year Roosevelt died, eighteen million dollars had been raised through the efforts of volunteers, and the foundation undertook the task of seeking the development of an anti-polio vaccine, which led in the 1950s to the success of the Salk vaccine and later the vaccine invented by Salk's major competitor, Albert Sabin.

In the years between 1924 and 1950, Warm Springs succeeded as a home to polios from all over the country, especially children, who wanted to become more than they were in both body and soul.

It was to this Warm Springs that I arrived in 1950, the summer I was eleven, in a village where the only four-term president of the United States was known as Doctor Roosevelt, where his vision for a hospital of polios living together like ordinary people had been realized.

These were the years before the massive public testing of the Salk vaccine in 1954, which would soon lead to the end of Warm Springs as a polio hospital. We were conscious that something like the smallpox vaccine might become available for polio, but I don't remember it as a subject of conversation.

I knew little of this until I started to write a book about my years at Warm Springs.

I have recurring memories of President Roosevelt, although I never met him. One features a flowered rug in our living room when I was a little girl, which had a stripe of white smeared across a loose-petaled rose. The white marked the place where my mother had thrown a bottle of nail polish remover at my father when he told her he had voted for Franklin Roosevelt in the 1936 presidential election. In another memory, I have a clear picture of myself lying on my stomach on a rug in the living room at the farm where we lived in Vienna, Virginia, my arms wrapped around the console radio, weeping as I listened to the coverage of President Roosevelt's funeral cortege leaving Warm Springs, where he had died at the Little White House on the afternoon of April 12, 1945. I was five, old enough to realize that I was listening to an important moment.

Soon after arriving for the first time at Warm Springs, I went with my family to the Little White House, the place Roosevelt built for himself in 1926 next to the grounds, to which he repaired as other presidents have done to their farms or ranches or estates or Camp David. It is a small and simple house, maintained as it was on the day he died, just after lunch, signing letters and a bill into law; he expected to join the children of Warm Springs at a party later that day. What struck me even then was that the house was so small, his bedroom spare and simple, the bed too short and narrow for a president.

But the image of Roosevelt that remains with perfect clarity is the dining room in Georgia Hall, which during my time at Warm Springs was where all the patients able to be moved from their hospital rooms gathered for special occasions. The tables were formally set and arranged in a U around a head table. I sat on the far edge of the room with the rest of the wheelchair children, but I could easily see, across the field of faces, a chair left vacant at the center of the head table.

Memory in Process

It is the middle of the night in Toledo, Ohio, and my father is at work broadcasting his weekly radio show, *Captain Reckless,* from WSPD, where he is the station manager. I am standing in my crib, holding on to the bars, calling for my mother, who has gotten out of bed and is on her way across the hall to my room. Her figure is backlit by the light in her bedroom.

I'm a year and a half old, recovering from paralytic poliomyelitis, and this is my first memory.

My mother is walking toward me in her long nightgown and it's winter. Behind her a man, taller than she is and very broad, is following her.

"Who's that man behind you, Mommy?" I ask as she comes into my room.

That is the full measure of the image in my head. My mother supplied the words.

"You called out to me in a low voice unlike your own," my mother would tell me over and over when I was young, and she was a literalist with a strong memory for narrative, her story always exactly the same.

"I was walking into your room and you weren't looking at me. You were looking just beyond, and you said, 'Who's that man behind you, Mommy?' And I must have screamed, because of course I thought you saw a man, but when I turned around, no one was there."

My father insisted that the man was in my imagination, but I remember seeing him, and he was a stranger.

Mid-August 1950, 96 Degrees

I WAS LYING in the back seat of our old lavender Chevrolet as it rattled south from Washington, D.C., along a two-lane highway toward Georgia, my feet hanging out of the open window. It was the first day of our journey, an empty moment out of time between leaving and arriving, and I was traveling in what felt like the absolute safety of isolation with my family locked together in the moving car. I had one arm flung across my eyes to block the morning sun of late summer, and in preparation for our destination, I was making a mental list of the things I knew for certain. It wasn't a list of the small things: what was in my blue and white bedroom, so I wouldn't forget how it looked while I was away, or the names of my friends or my stash of trading cards or the movies I'd seen or the boys I loved. Those were lists I would make later in the year, in the wide-lined spiral notebook I kept in my bedside drawer and wrote in under the covers after lights out.

No, that morning on the road to Georgia I was thinking of the serious things.

I knew, for example, that it was easy to die.

Even at eleven I felt a kind of urgency, as if we were all hurrying to some unknown destination. Against that finality, I had prayed every night since I could remember to the first star I saw in the black sky. *Star light, star bright, first star I see tonight, I wish I may, I wish I might, have the wish I wish tonight. That my small family of four and General Beauregard and Grandma Richards will live happily ever after.*

Our small family lived in a state of emergency that in retrospect

was a state of mind. My father had grown up poor in New Philadelphia, Ohio. His father had died by the time he was ten, and his
mother was employed until she was in her seventies, selling costume jewelry at the local five-and-ten. Local, by the late 1920s, was
Urbana, another small town in Ohio, where my father met my
mother. He decided on her in spite of her age, which was older;
her upbringing, which gave her access to the country club; and
her refusal to accept the frequent gifts he left on the front porch
of her house, returning them promptly to his mother's tiny apartment.

When, on a night in November of 1937, my father, by then a
crime reporter at the *Cincinnati Post,* crashed the Urbana Country Club, my mother was dancing with her new fiancé. My father
cut in, dancing — and he was a smooth, graceful dancer — to the
end of the song before he was escorted out of the club.

They were married two months later, on New Year's Day, in the
living room of my mother's house on College Street.

The night of the wedding, my parents set out for Cincinnati, to
take up residence in a hotel for retired and unemployed actors. I
have a photograph of my mother in that hotel, taken in the dark,
her hands around a lighted globe illuminating her face. There
must have been some kind of séance going on, and she is conjur-
ing or playing the role of conjurer. The expression in her eyes is
otherworldly. I keep it in my kitchen as evidence of the lovely
mystery that their marriage was to me and the stage on which our
lives seemed, in my child's mind, to be played out before an imagined audience. There was a delicate sense of drama between them.

On the way from Urbana to Cincinnati, driving at night, my father noticed in the circle of the car's headlights a paper bag lying
on the side of the road. As the story goes — the one they chose to
tell again and again to define what they wanted us to know about
the nature of their marriage — my father pulled over and jumped
out of the car, calling behind him that he believed there was a
baby in the paper bag. Through the passenger-side window, my

mother watched as he hurried over to the bag, which was barely moving in the night wind. He picked it up and looked inside.

My mother, whimsical but literal-minded, was just getting to know this man she had married that afternoon, but she had no reason to doubt there was a baby. And by temperament she was a willing believer.

She patted down the skirt she had made for her honeymoon trousseau to be ready for the baby when my father returned with it.

"What happened?" she must have asked my father when he dropped the empty paper bag in the back seat.

He slid into the driver's seat, put the car in gear, and accelerated.

"There could have been a baby," he said crossly as he pulled back onto the highway, headed toward Cincinnati.

"Yes," she agreed, "there could have been."

She must have been bewildered by the strangeness of my father's imagination, and fascinated too, and thrilled to be on a car trip during which such a thing might happen.

My father was not conventionally handsome, but he was compelling and charismatic. In his twenties, he was wiry and balding, with a half-moon of black hair at the base of his skull, a prominent nose, small bones, black eyes, and an easy way of moving. My friends had crushes on him. To us as children — and he died before we had a chance to know him as adults — he was thrilling, with an unerring instinct for narrative, a sharp wit, and a dark, delicious sense of humor. The rooms of our small house were bright with heat when he was in them.

He had a crime reporter's mentality, a poor boy's sense of mortality, and I think an abiding fear, even an expectation, of losing what he loved. Especially my mother.

He filled the house with a needy crowd: lonely, down-on-their-luck, out-of-work journalists; soldiers, when the war was on; stray cats he found on the streets of scummy wartime Washington; and the occasional lost dog. I was attracted to him and frightened too, and the fear wasn't of what he might do or say, although we were not spared his wit. It had to do with how quickly he could ignite. How much I was ignited in his presence.

But I was in love with my mother.

In the front seat of the lavender Chevrolet, my parents were talking the way they did when my father was driving, his hands together at the bottom of the steering wheel, my mother leaning into him so her soft butter-brown curls brushed his cheek. On the radio, "Tennessee Waltz" was playing, and my father started to sing it: "I was waltzing with my darlin' . . ." I knew all the words.

On the floor of the back seat, my brother was zooming his metal cars over his plastic soldiers until all the soldiers were dead and bloody. From time to time he'd lift his head from the carnage to tell us he was about to throw up, and then he'd return to war.

My brother was five years younger than I, and that year and for a long time afterward, I liked him much better than he liked me. He may not have been sufficient to my idea of the proper size for a family, but he was all I had, and he was mine — although I wished I had more brothers and that I was the one girl in the middle of a squadron of them, instead of being one of two siblings with a lukewarm reputation as a sister.

"Will you live in the hospital forever?" Jeffrey had asked while we were packing up the car for the trip to Georgia in front of our yellow stucco house in Cleveland Park. He was curious but not concerned.

"Nothing is forever," I replied, irritated that my absence was being greeted with something like enthusiasm.

"I am forever," Jeffrey said with confidence.

He was almost six years old that summer. An easy baby, a perfect little boy, winsome, sweet, the right amount of shy.

"No trouble," my mother would say happily. "Jeffie is no trouble at all."

That was the word out on my little brother when we were growing up.

I don't remember feeling jealous, and I don't believe I was. But I did understand that if Jeffie was no trouble, I was certainly trouble enough for two.

When the time came for me to run away from home, I was six and Jeffrey was a year old and we lived in a row house in Georgetown on a busy street. I don't know what occasioned my decision to bolt that particular spring day, but I do remember standing in the doorway to the living room watching my brother play quietly in his playpen while upstairs my mother was taking a bath. I made a plan then to walk out the front door, take my Radio Flyer wagon parked in the tiny yard, and walk to the village of Georgetown, where I would get on a streetcar with the wagon and disappear into the world.

I imagined my mother calling me when she got out of the bath and I wouldn't be there to answer. She would wrap a towel around herself and rush downstairs, but I'd be gone and Jeffrey would be gripping the side of the playpen, looking at her with his mournful blue eyes. It was my hope that she'd be *beside herself with worry,* as she might say, that she'd put in an emergency call to my father, phone the police, rush upstairs to dress, run downstairs and out the front door in search of me, leaving my brother to sit in his playpen, *good as gold, a perfect angel,* waiting for her return.

But it must have occurred to me that she might be relieved to find me gone. That she'd lie down on the couch in the living room in a state of quiet bliss, wrapped in her towel, her wet hair spread out on the pillow, singing the sweet old-fashioned songs she liked to sing.

On second thought, I picked Jeffrey up, opened the front door, closed it softly behind me, put the baby in the Radio Flyer, where he sat with his small hands folded in his lap, and I took off up P Street on my way to Wisconsin Avenue and the streetcar to nowhere.

I was picked up by the police before I reached the avenue, but I had already walked five blocks and crossed four streets. When the policeman with my mother brought us home, my father was standing outside on the street, his face white with terror.

"Do you want to know why I took Jeffrey when I ran away from home?" I asked when my father came to my bedroom door to tell me goodnight later that evening.

"I don't want to know why," he said. "You did what you did."

Unlike other of our family stories, that one did not get told over and over. I assume my father understood exactly why I took my baby brother, but it wasn't a subject for his consideration.

We were a family given to a certain amount of unsparing truth and to considerable secrecy. Negotiating the land mines in between required a careful step I never quite achieved.

I was a *bad* child. That was my perception of myself. I remember reading once about the strange attractor, a star that unsettles the planetary balance, which was the role I seemed to play in our family life. For one, I was always getting sick. And not just a little sick, either, in those days when most of the penicillin had been sent overseas for the soldiers. I was at the center of my parents' world and had every reason to trust their love, but I also knew that my life had stood in the way of theirs. I felt accountable, as if my illness were premeditated. As if I intended to make things difficult, or had too little moral strength to resist.

Children who are ill *know* this about themselves. They aren't blind to the pain and trouble their illness causes the people who love them. And I can imagine even in my own mother a silent exhaustion, a growing irritation, at what had befallen her young life, her brand-new marriage, in the first four years of mine.

I had polio when I was a baby living in Toledo, where my father was the manager of WSPD radio. We moved to Washington, D.C., when the Office of Censorship was established, after Pearl Harbor, and my father was asked to direct its radio division. When I was four, living in a small, cold house in Silver Spring, Maryland, which my father filled with soldiers on their way through Washington to war, I had rheumatic fever. I spent that winter in bed, my mother sitting beside me playing out the stories of the daytime soaps with paper dolls. Outside my window, my naked doll Ann Shirley, named for the dimpled, curly-haired movie idol Shirley Temple, her golden hair matted with filth, her plaster skin peeling, lay on the frozen ground where I'd asked my mother to put her so she could catch pneumonia. Which she finally must have done, since one day she was gone.

And when I was five, in the autumn of 1944, the October my brother was born, I caught spinal meningitis, in an outbreak that filled the Children's Ward of Washington's Providence Hospital with lines of children in metal beds, many of them dying. Sickness has a peculiar glamour. I was both trouble and the center of the universe.

The Christmas after I had meningitis was a happy one for my parents. We had moved out of Silver Spring to a farm in Vienna, Virginia, and they had a baby boy and dogs and chickens and ducks and cows and a horse, and I was recuperating, which they never thought I'd get to do. In celebration, although it may not sound celebratory, my parents filled my stocking with coal on Christmas Eve.

I am my parents' child, so I understand why they did that — in the spirit of fun and relief and for a big old laugh at death. I'm sure they intended to include me in the joke and must have thought I had a more sophisticated sense of humor than I did.

I didn't cry. I thought that I deserved the coal.

"Are you scared?" my brother asked, climbing up on the back seat beside me.

"I'm not scared," I told him, and probably meant it. "The next time you see me, I'm going to be a different girl."

"What kind of girl?" he asked.

"A perfect one," I said.

I believed that all it would take for my transformation from bad to good was an act of will, as if will had its own independent life separate from the self and could be fashioned of whatever mate-rial you had at hand.

What I felt on that long, hot drive to Georgia was a kind of wild exhilaration, not for the young girl arriving at Warm Springs that August of 1950, but for the one I expected to become by the time I left, a reconstructed girl unimaginable at that moment in my daily life.

In June, I had completed fifth grade at Sidwell Friends, a Quaker school that had excellent academics, an ethic of service in keeping with Quaker philosophy, and a willingness, unlike the public schools, to accept handicapped children. Which is why I was there. I think the school had every hope that I'd be a star pupil to compensate for my handicap, but I was neither a star pupil nor a star citizen. On the Character side of my report card, I failed Cooperation, Re-sponsibility, Obedience, Discipline, everything but Initiative.

And Initiative can have many interpretations, not all of them good.

A letter accompanying my final grades that year requested that I not return to Friends after my stint at Warm Springs, since I should be well enough to attend a public school like everybody else.

In the back seat of the Chevrolet on the second leg of our journey south, the day we were due to arrive at Warm Springs, I lay with my arm covering my eyes to shut out my brother's war game, which he was playing on my legs, my stomach, and up and down the back doors of the car.

I was thinking of rehabilitation. Not the kind for which I was going to the hospital. I expected the doctors and nurses and phys-ical therapists to take care of my paralyzed leg, expected I'd walk out of the hospital free of crutches and braces, looking like Mar-garet O'Brien, my particular choice, the pigtailed darling of late-forties movies with two long, beautiful legs, thick hair that waved when she took it out of plaits, and plump bow lips. Almost a conventional beauty but not quite, which is exactly where I wanted to place myself in the lineup.

Since the doctors were planning to transplant muscles and stabilize bones, it seemed quite possible that everything in my whole physical biography would improve.

The rehabilitation I had in mind was of myself.

At the end of my mother's life — my parents' lives were much too short — she kept aphorisms for self-improvement on the fridge: "Smile and the world smiles with you. Cry and you cry alone." "Pack up your troubles in your old kit bag and smile, smile, smile." "A good deed a day keeps the doctor away."

It was surprising in my mother, these Hallmark platitudes. She was too whimsical, I thought at the time, too eccentric for that kind of pedestrian belief. I wondered whether she hadn't always been quietly about the business of turning her own sadness into some defined act of self-betterment. She was the most gentle and sweet person I have ever known. I cannot imagine that she believed there was a need for improvement or that she struggled with a sense of failure, but she must have. And by some form of osmosis, this need had been communicated to me by the time I reached Warm Springs.

In the back seat with my eyes closed, I examined my transgressions, making a plan for daily improvements. It was my goal to emerge from Warm Springs reinvented as a faultless girl. I saw my future self as no longer the perpetrator of accidents but as an angel of God.

Taking off my shoes so the hot wind blew on my toes as the car sped down the highway, I rewound the reel of fifth grade that I had completed in June.

Mrs. Gosnell was my teacher. She was a squat, humorless woman with gray hair who had a bad temper and an uncontrollable dislike for me.

And the perfect Toni Brewer, with her looping braids and impeccable demeanor, was the girl I planned to be at the end of my initiation at Warm Springs.

The arrival of Harold Ickes in my fifth-grade year at Friends changed my life. He was my first genuine friend. I had had other friends, but they were either not real friends at all or sympathy friends, either mine for them or theirs for me.

Harold was mine.

In the late forties, children were seldom home-schooled, but fifth grade was Harold's first year in an actual classroom. He had lived on a farm outside Washington, lived freely and without a lot of social contact with kids his age. He was the son of an older father, who was secretary of the interior under President Roosevelt, and a strong-minded mother, and he had no interest in the order of school or the requirements and limitations and fussiness of it. He came along at just the right time for me. We both were smart enough but were poor students, failures on the Character side of our report cards with plans of our own.

At one point or another, probably late in the year, after our general academic failures were widely known in the class, thanks to the loose-lipped Mrs. Gosnell, we decided it would be a good idea to break the monotony of silence in Quaker Meeting by shooting off cap guns.

It wasn't a careless decision. We had Quaker Meeting once a week with the whole school, and daily in our own class we had a Moment of Silence. We were well aware — it was impossible not to be — that the Quakers believed in decisions arrived at by consensus and in peace and that they refused to participate in war. Quaker Meetings were silent and long, and a cap gun seemed to provide the opportunity for a short, emphatic statement.

I can't remember what happened to Harold, but I know that I was sent home for a few days to consider what I'd done.

The day I came back, Mrs. Gosnell stood in front of the room and called for the usual Moment of Silence.

"We all know that Suzie Richards has caused a lot of trouble this year," she began. "But we must feel sorry for her because she has a crippled leg."

At the small hotel in Warm Springs, where we stayed the last night before I went into the hospital, I slept on the floor. My mother and father and Jeffrey slept in the double bed, and it was intended that I sleep with them.

"I'm too hot," I said.

"But it's your last night with us," Jeffrey said in a sentimental moment.

I watched them with longing, all curled up together in the bed under a slow-moving fan. But I wasn't going to test my emotional strength by giving in to the comfort of their warm bodies.

"I'm still too hot," I said. "I need to sleep by myself."

Dr. Nicholson, Sister Kenny,
My Mother, and Me

MY MOTHER PLANNED to stay at Warm Springs for a month. My father and Jeffrey would fly home after my first surgery, which was scheduled for the Thursday morning after my admission on Monday. Grandma Richards would help my father with Jeffrey, who would be going into first grade in September, and my mother would return to Washington at the end of September, at the earliest.

"This will be an adventure," my mother said. "I'll stay for a while and then I'll go back home and you'll have a wonderful time."

I believed her. I believed everything she told me.

My pediatrician in Toledo had diagnosed my poliomyelitis as paralytic strep throat. It was not uncommon to misdiagnose polio; I was among many, including Roosevelt, whose initial diagnosis had to do with inflammatory disease or a serious back problem or one of the strep-related illnesses. My mother had never heard of this particular strep condition — perhaps it existed, perhaps not — but she was told that the paralysis would be gone as soon as the streptococcus bacteria disappeared. By the time my parents discovered that I had had polio, not strep, the virus was gone and the residual damage remained, as it does with polio.

The damage was to the right side of my body: I had been left with traces of muscles on my right side, especially in my leg, but I was unable to walk after the virus disappeared. I was, however, very young and had been walking only a short time before I got polio, so my mother figured she could do something about my condition. As soon as I was better, she devised a military regimen of exercises to coax those muscles back to life.

The illness caused by the polio virus is similar to influenza, beginning with a high fever, aching muscles and head, and lethargy. If the particular virus — which is spread through feces, entering the system through the mouth and eventually lodging in the spinal fluid — is the one that causes paralytic polio, then the limbs become first numb, then painful, and over hours or days the body is gradually paralyzed from the neck down. If the virus is bulbar polio, then the patient's diaphragm is paralyzed, and he must be placed in an iron lung in order to breathe. After the illness runs its course, a few or many or all of the muscles affected return to a measure of use. More children than adults were victims of polio, more boys than girls, and it was believed that a high level of physical activity at the onset of illness — as happened with Roosevelt, for example — led to greater paralysis. Whether or not that was ultimately proven true, infants generally had milder cases of paralytic polio, and I had polio as an infant.

My mother and I spent days together, all through my childhood, on the floor, on the bed, standing against the wall, doing a long series of exercises. She made a game of this routine, so it felt pretty much like play to me. I'd spend hours standing pencil-straight against a wall — like a soldier guarding the queen of England, she'd say, or the Nutcracker Prince (with the *Nutcracker Suite* playing in the background), or the tin soldier from *The Wizard of Oz* — or like me when I grew up to be a spy, listening at the door to the enemy's conversation. My mother would hold me against the wall so I wouldn't fall while I prepared for the Olympic Games, balancing a book on top of my head, or while I tried out for the lead puppet in a dance of marionettes. I would sit on the end of a chair, my foot in her hand, while she massaged and exercised each tiny muscle in my toes and feet and ankles, my neck and hands and arms. By playing the role of a patient, I was preparing to be an orthopedic physician, a nurse on a battlefield of injured soldiers, a fallen Olympic runner. She had me do stretches, my foot against her hand, my leg against her arm.

I was always in the process of inventing someone I wasn't, someone I might become.

Our days, which to an outside observer like my father seemed long and tedious, were full of surprises, in spite of the repeated exercises. What would my mother imagine next for us? For me?

That first winter, when I was too young to remember, we went to Florida and stayed in a guesthouse. My mother made a party of it, bringing my aunt and cousin along so we could all escape the gloomy Ohio weather. I have pictures of myself at the beach with her. She is holding me around my stomach, swishing me through the water. I'm riding on her back in the shallows near shore. She had hoped the sand would serve as a brace and I could learn to walk in Florida, that the sun would restore my health.

By the time we moved to Washington, D.C., when I was almost three, I could walk in braces, holding my mother's hand or swinging back and forth in a kind of jump step, moving forward by throwing my hips ahead of me.

Washington was a damp, disease-ridden swamp city toward the end of the Second World War. Poverty and illness were widespread; the city and its suburbs were teeming with soldiers, stuffed into apartments and rooming houses and spare bedrooms in people's homes, like ours in Silver Spring. Rats and rabid dogs ran in the streets, and hospitals were overcrowded. There was a shortage of doctors and nurses, and in the absence of penicillin disease was rampant: scarlet fever, spinal meningitis, polio. Polio was the plague for the parents of that generation, lurking in the shadows, sweeping in with symptoms of influenza that could, in a matter of hours, paralyze or kill a child.

Signs warning of scarlet fever were plastered on the doors and windows of houses where we lived. I got rheumatic fever before my mother had even found a doctor in our new city. Dr. Margaret

Mary Nicholson was the only pediatrician willing to make house calls at night during the war. She came from downtown, what is now called the Old City, on her bicycle in a white dress, with hair pinned to the top of her head in a loopy bun that sometimes gave way and fell to her waist, with a stethoscope around her neck, a crucifix in her pocket. The treatment was ten Hail Marys, kale sandwiches on brown bread, and cod liver oil. She came every day for weeks and weeks until I got well.

She was famous in Washington for taking care of the city's poor. At a time when blacks couldn't go to the hospitals in segregated Washington, she'd pick up the sickest babies in her bicycle basket, haul them to the hospital, treat them herself in the emergency room, and take them home. She ran her office like a clinic, with mothers and children lining the halls, sitting on the floor, waiting sometimes for hours and hours. I didn't leave Dr. Nicholson until I was twenty-one years old, got married, and moved to England. She'd stay in her office, often into the night, until everyone in the line had been seen, charging what a family could pay, or nothing. And she always had plans in the works, for orphans in Mexico, for leukemia patients in the Deep South, for burn victims. She liked my mother, and somehow — I never asked and don't know how it happened — they were in cahoots. Whatever wild scheme Dr. Nicholson had in mind in the years when I was very young, my mother was part of its execution.

Dr. Nicholson's plan for me was that I should be the subject of a lecture by the renowned Sister Kenny, in the amphitheater of Washington's Doctors Hospital, in front of hundreds of physicians and residents and interns and nurses.

Sister Elizabeth Kenny, a physical therapist without formal medical training, was controversial in the medical establishment and enormously popular elsewhere for her method of treating infantile paralysis. When she had been a bush nurse in the Australian outback, she came across a young girl who was paralyzed, her body stiff and contorted. Sister Kenny decided instinctively that the paralysis and stiffness were due to muscle spasms and devised a treatment of hot packs — strips of wool soaked in boiling water — which she used to help the muscles to relax. She then "reeducated" the muscles by manipulation to function correctly. She dismissed the notion that polio was a disease of the nerves and the belief held by scientists that its residual paralysis was a result of nerve damage. Nevertheless, her method of therapy was often very successful.

In the forties, she traveled around the United States, treating patients, making speeches, arguing the case for her hot-pack treatment, and seeking funding and support from the medical community, which generally shunned her.

By 1945 she was a celebrity, and Dr. Nicholson wanted her to examine me. She especially wanted Sister Kenny to see the method my mother had used in restoring to use some of the paralyzed muscles on my right side.

The morning of my first stage appearance, my mother showed me a picture of Sister Kenny on the front page of that day's newspaper.

"She's very famous, you see."

My idea of famous was a movie star, but she didn't appear like one to me. Sister Kenny looked large and old and fierce, but I was unworried. I was wearing my new clothes, my hair curled for the occasion, and my mother's voice as she explained what would happen at the hospital was contagious with excitement for my leading role.

Perhaps my mother was susceptible to Dr. Nicholson's insistence that Sister Kenny would want to know her method. My guess in retrospect, however, is that Dr. Nicholson, whom I thought of as a kind of Mary Poppins as she pedaled around Washington, her white dress flying behind her, pockets full of lollipops, a baby bouncing in her wire basket, was competitive with Sister Kenny. She didn't want a nonmedical professional riding high on slim evidence, and so she was challenging the Australian saint in a serious public forum.

That morning, riding in the back of a taxicab downtown to the hospital, my mother and I were gleeful stage-struck innocents, holding hands, swinging with the cab around the curves of Rock Creek Parkway on our way to victory.

Dr. Nicholson met us in front of the hospital with her bicycle, slipped a lollipop into my jacket pocket, told me to repeat the usual ten Hail Marys and the Our Father, which she had taught me to say, made me stick out my tongue so she could see if it was coated, checked my fingernails for white spots, and asked me how much I had in my piggy bank for the poor children in Guatemala. As far as I knew, my mother never took exception to anything Dr. Nicholson asked of me, including reciting Catholic prayers.

We followed Dr. Nicholson down a long corridor and into a room where another child with polio was lying on a stretcher, covered with a sheet.

My mother lifted me up, took off my clothes, and folded them on a chair. A nurse put me in a hospital gown and covered me with a sheet.

"You'll be wheeled into the theater by a nurse," Dr. Nicholson said. "Your mother and I will be in front-row seats — if you turn your head, you'll be able to see us. Sister Kenny will look at your bad leg and your neck and the right side of your body, and you will lie still and let her look."

There was no gentle hand of Dr. Nicholson on my arm, no soft words or kisses, just her steady presence and high expectations.

That morning, my mother was wearing a broad-brimmed black cloth hat with a thin, red-striped silk ribbon around the crown. When I looked over to check whether she was in the amphitheater, as the nurse pushed my stretcher onto the stage under the bright lights, she was sitting in the first row next to Dr. Nicholson. She looked very beautiful. She always did.

I didn't see Sister Kenny until I was directly beside her. She was looking at the audience, and from the stretcher, with my angle of perspective slightly skewed, what I saw was an enormous woman who looked like a man, with a boxy jaw and a booming voice and hands the size of a trucker's. I recently looked at a photograph of Sister Kenny on the Internet: she had wide-set eyes, a pretty mouth, an undistinguished jaw, and a pleasant expression. She was probably eighteen in the photograph, and that morning she was sixty-five.

"My name is Susan Richards," I said, as Dr. Nicholson had instructed me.

Sister Kenny looked down and lifted the sheet — or, rather, in a grand gesture tore it off my body, in its oversized hospital gown.

"This is patient Susan Richards, age five, infantile paralysis, November 1941, paralytic polio with residual paralysis on the right side, atrophy of the leg, seriously deformed right foot."

She looked at my legs, my hips, checked my arms, wiggled my ankles and toes, all the time shaking her head back and forth with an expression of despair.

"The patient has been treated by methods devised by her mother. These methods have never included the application of hot cloths or muscle stretching or reeducation of the damaged muscles. And so . . ." She lifted me off the stretcher in a swoop, set me on the ground where I wavered unsteadily, and said, "Walk."

I did walk. I didn't fall, and it seemed to me I walked in a straight enough line, but I must not have taken more than five or six steps before she lifted me back onto the stretcher and raised her hands in a gesture of defeat.

"By the time she is twelve years old, this child will not be able to walk any longer."

There was a commotion in the audience, and out of nowhere Dr. Nicholson flew up, gathered me in her arms, rushed across the stage, took off my hospital gown, dressed me in my tights and dress, buttoned up my overcoat, tied my hat on, and delivered me to my mother.

"Ten Hail Marys, Susan. Quickly."

In a matter of seconds we were rushing down the corridor, my hand in my mother's, out the front door, hailing a cab, and seated side by side in the back, looping through Rock Creek Park.

I had let my mother down.

She took off her broad-brimmed hat, put it in her lap, and gripped my hand tightly as we swung through the park.

"I am so sorry," she said, turning to face me.

"For what?" I asked, confused that she should be the one who was sorry.

"For what Sister Kenny said to you."

"I didn't believe Sister Kenny," I said, and in the dark safety of the back seat of the taxi, under a canopy of budding trees, I leaned hard against her. "You told me I could walk, and I can."

The Ticket of Admission

THE MORNING I WAS admitted to Warm Springs was cool enough for my mother to wear the yellow linen suit she had made for this occasion, copying the design, as she did with her clothes, from the French edition of *Vogue*. She had hoped to be a dress designer, but the years she would have started a career were those between the end of the Depression and World War II, so dress designing gave way to teaching school, and then to me.

Nobody I knew in Washington, D.C., had a mother who looked like mine did. It thrilled me to walk beside her, knowing that people were staring at us.

"What a beautiful woman," they would be thinking. "And the child holding her hand must be her daughter."

I felt almost pretty by association.

But this morning in Warm Springs, Georgia, arriving for the first time at the hospital that would be my home, I wanted anonymity.

When I got out of the car in the parking lawn and looked across the lawn to the hospital, I could suddenly imagine myself living here, careening up and down the walkways, in and out of the buildings, here and there with my new friends, nothing to do except hang around together, stretched on our backs in the sun, drinking Coca-Colas and whispering secrets back and forth. There would be no school; my mother had assured me of that.

The hospital — and we called it Warm Springs, not the hospital — was very grand. Not the institution I had expected, more like a hotel than a hospital, like the spa it had once been at the turn of the century. White-painted brick buildings surrounding a wide expanse of lawn, with trees and flowers, winding cement walkways, the southern calm of a balmy afternoon.

In the distance, as we made our way down the path to the admissions building, patients were crossing the courtyard in wheelchairs, coming out of the buildings, moving along with purpose, stopping on the lawn to talk.

I'd have a wheelchair myself, I thought. I'd never had my own wheelchair. I'd never needed one.

I constructed a particular self at a very early age. I can only imagine the process now. As a child often sick, often in bed, I spent a lot of time watching from the window as other children played. If I wanted to command the attention of visitors to my room so they'd want to stay with me, I would have to be engaging and uncomplaining and cheerful, full of stories to detain them. With little going on in my own life except games with my mother, I made up the stories, a mix of what I listened to on daytime soaps and what swam as fantasy through my mind. My mother would sit at the end of my bed, her chin in her hand, listening to everything I had to tell her with rapt attention and delight, as the lines between invention and fact bled into one another like watercolors and became something entirely new.

For my sometimes melancholic mother, for whom I felt myself to be a source of so much trouble, I needed to be sunshine, equal to her sacrifice for me.

When I think now of how attached I was to my mother, it is notable that I told her so little bad news. I could be an edgy child, hot-tempered, but my outbursts were swift to come and go. I didn't complain. In general I was happy, as she reported to me later and as I remember. And who wouldn't be happy as a little girl with her mother's full attention? To her mind, I had the genetic good fortune of a sunny disposition. Things didn't bother me, she'd tell her friends; my illnesses caused me little of the psychic or physical pain that they might have done in another, more sensitive child, one less able to *roll with the punches,* as my father said of me.

I didn't realize until I was in my twenties, and a mother myself, that the happy-go-lucky, fearless girl she and I had needed to believe in had been an invention for both of us.

Georgia Hall was the main administration building at Warm Springs. On that first morning, I walked through its doors some distance in front of my parents, less wary than determined. Perhaps I smiled at people in the waiting room, a habit I had developed for these situations.

"Speak first," my mother had always told me, knowing that a bony child on crutches with the dark demeanor of a war survivor might not be well received. "Say 'I'm Susan Richards' and smile and reach out your hand." I was probably three or four when these lessons in survival began. I never questioned my mother's insistence on them, a result of her own shyness and the disapproving looks she received from people on the street who saw me as a damaged child, some unspoken comment on her failure as a mother.

The waiting room was crowded with new patients like me checking into the hospital early on a Monday morning. I wondered whether they would all be staying as long as I would. And whether we'd soon, in a matter of days or weeks, be friends.

The subject of the length of my stay was fuzzy. It was August, and I knew I'd be able to go home for Thanksgiving, that I'd have one surgery initially and be in a cast for a while and then have physical therapy. All that before Thanksgiving and then I'd go home. Perhaps I'd get to stay at home through Christmas and return for other surgeries. Or maybe not. "Depending on how things go" was the way the doctors had spoken to my mother and father about it. It was my plan to leave the hospital at Thanksgiving and not return. I figured I could rehabilitate myself by then, but I didn't tell my parents about it.

I walked into the waiting room with the kind of confidence that comes of an overdeveloped imagination short on critical review. I was the girl of the hour, that's how I remember it, and that's the way I had intended to present myself in this room of crippled children.

I had daydreamed this scene for years.

I'd known about Warm Springs since I was seven and had gone to the Cleveland Clinic to see a famous orthopedic doctor, who recommended the hospital to my parents. He thought I should go immediately for surgery.

"Don't wait," he said.

My mother waited. It was her intuition that if I had surgery before I was more fully developed, it might interrupt the growing bone. Doctors did not agree with her. No precedent, they said, for bone surgery stopping the growth of a child's bones. But my mother had more confidence in intuition than in facts, and she was stubborn. Every year I had my hand x-rayed to determine how close I was to my full growth. The x-ray taken before my eleventh birthday was promising, and so it was arranged that I would go to Warm Springs at that soft moment between childhood and adolescence. It would be an easy time to be out of school; I wouldn't miss all that much.

As it turned out, my mother was correct about bones. I was two and a half inches short of my full growth when I was eleven, and the initial surgery did in fact stop the growth of my right leg: I am five feet four inches standing on one foot and five feet one and a half inches on the other. The difference in the length of my legs at seven years of age would have been more than a foot.

I'd thought about Warm Springs for a long time and imagined my perfect life there. My triumph, as I imagined it, was about to begin.

The hard-backed chairs circled the room, and most of them were filled. A baby boy maybe ten months old, with a big head and floppy body, was sitting on his mother's lap. Two girls with their parents, the parents talking back and forth, sat next to the baby boy. One of the girls had a back brace, like a corset, over her yellow pinafore and two long leg braces locked at the knee, sticking straight out. The second girl, who smiled shyly at me when I sat down, was in a wheelchair with a contraption attached, and her arms rested in slings hanging by thin chains. A grown man was lying on a stretcher, his head turned away from a woman, perhaps his wife, whose hand rested on his forehead. In the corner of the room there was a boy of about twelve, maybe thirteen, whom I'd soon come to know as Joey Buckley. He had a mass of black, curly hair, with a knitted cap and a cigarette poking out from behind his ear.

I included him immediately in the vision I had for my new life.

He was sitting in a wheelchair, an older man beside him wearing a red flannel shirt in the middle of August, the sleeves pushed up, his bare elbows on his knees, his head in his hands.

I walked through the middle of the crowded room, past the chairs already taken on either side, past the admissions desk, where a long-legged red-haired woman was talking on the telephone. I moved quickly, conscious of my speed, in braces without crutches, swinging my leg forward from the hip like a wind-up toy, winning this footrace with practiced posture — straight back, level shoulders, tucked chin.

These small accomplishments would be recognized and admired by my new teammates.

"Stand like a dancer," my mother would tell me at home as I flattened my back against the wall, a book balancing sideways on my head. "Pretend you are a dancer."

And you will be was the suggestion in her voice, but she was careful not to promise the impossible, only to let me know what opportunities might be in store if I kept to my regime.

My parents and my reluctant brother, who had spent a lot of his early childhood waiting for me to be examined in such rooms as this one, had followed me in and taken a seat next to the older man with Joey Buckley. I stood alone at a distance, assessing my future.

I don't particularly like to be alone now. I often prefer a coffee-house full of strangers to my own study, or a friend in the guest bed to an empty house when my husband is working in another city.

But by the time I was eleven, I had spent long hours alone and knew the benefits — that a certain kind of courage was easier to come by alone, that I was more alert, my senses sharper, my vision in particular, and that as a solitary girl I would put myself forward in ways that wouldn't be necessary in the company of my parents.

I lowered the blinds of my eyes so the waiting patients wouldn't notice that I was checking them out. All of them were young, with the exception of the man on the stretcher. I began to realize that every one of the children old enough to walk was in a wheel-chair.

So they couldn't walk. I registered that fact with a sudden sink-ing of confidence. Seven children, and I was the only one who could walk.

In my daydreams of this adventure, I was coming home to a place where everyone would be exactly like me, a place where I'd be known for my own self and not for polio.

At Sidwell Friends School, especially as I got older, I'd answered to the name "Gimp" as if it were my own.

When I was four or five, my mother sent me in braces to Ma-dame LaFrere's Ballet School, expecting that Madame LaFrere would be agreeable to a dancer in orthopedic shoes gripping the barre. Handicapped was not a word in my vocabulary. I was ex-pected to participate. And when Madame LaFrere said it was *eemposseeble* for me to do ballet, my mother set up a barre in my bedroom so she and I could dance together.

I played sports, always the last one chosen for the team, whether I could play the sport or not. Volleyball, soccer, and soft-ball, all were possible for me to play, and in fact a peg leg has a pogo-stick quality that an ordinary leg lacks, so I bounced along. I could have been a student, but I didn't have any interest in academics, so I hitched my wagon to sports. Of course, in any real sense, I didn't belong there. Nevertheless.

At night I'd lie in bed and think with relief about this place of crippled children and what it would be like to live there.

At Warm Springs I would be one among equals.

I sat down next to Joey Buckley and told him my name.

He shrugged.

"Did you just get here?" he asked without introducing himself.

"Last night. We drove for two days and nights."

"We drove up this morning from Alabama."

His voice was soft and rolling and I liked the sound of it.

"I came here because I'm going to be a football player at Alabama in a few years and I've got to get ready for it."

"You're not going to be any football player with that cigarette behind your ear, Joey."

The man in the flannel shirt lifted his head, leaned back, and gave me a look, not unfriendly but not smiling either.

"I don't smoke the cigarette, Papa," Joey said. "I keep it behind my ear because I like the way it looks."

"You're not going to be a football player anyway," his father said. "You can't walk. Got that, son?"

"I came here to learn how," Joey said without looking at his father. "What about you?" he asked me.

"I came here for some operations," I said, adding an operation or two in my head just to keep abreast of the crowd in the waiting room.

"Me too. They're going to lock my ankles so they don't buckle when I stand up, and then they'll find some muscles and put them in my legs because all the ones I have are dead, and when I get out of here, I'll be standing and I'll have these muscles and pretty soon when I practice a lot, I'll be able to walk."

Joey's father gave a long, noisy sigh, leaned his head back, and looked at the ceiling.

"My dad doesn't think it's going to happen," Joey said. "He's not in my body so he doesn't know what I can do."

"You're right, son," his father said. "I'm not in your body. And I wish I were so we could trade and you could play football."

"You couldn't play football now, Papa."

"You never know. Maybe I could," his father said, and I was glad to see my father lean in and engage Mr. Buckley in a conversation about football at Alabama.

"Are you scared?" Joey asked.

"Nope. What about you?"

"I don't get scared," he said. "I've had polio a long time, since I was eight years old, so now I won't look like I have it anymore, right?"

"Right," I said, and I believed him.

"I got this from my cousin Pete, who's worse off than me. He'll never walk, that's what the doctor told his mother. He can't even come to Warm Springs because it wouldn't do him a bit of good."

"I got it when I was one, so I don't know how I caught it."

He was looking at me, and I could tell he wanted to ask me a question but didn't know exactly how to do it.

"I don't smoke, if that's what you were wondering," he said.

Out of the corner of my eye, I checked his legs. I wanted to ask him if he really couldn't walk.

He was sitting in a leather and aluminum wheelchair, quite a spiffy one, and wearing two long leg braces, unlocked so his knees bent. On the back of the chair he had a set of crutches attached by a leather band.

"So you *can* walk," I said, indicating the crutches.

"A little with crutches but not so good. I can stand if I lock my braces," he said, "and I can swing my legs on crutches but not for long." He lifted one leg and locked the brace. "So my dad would say I can't really walk."

"I guess most kids here can't."

"Looks like that," he said. "And you can, right?"

I drew a deep breath.

"Actually," I said quietly, so my parents couldn't hear and have to speak to me later about lying, which my mother would certainly have done, "I look like I'm a lot better off than I really am."

I decided to ask for a wheelchair before I left the waiting room.

Suddenly, after years of longing to walk with ease and run and skate and ride a bike, I had changed my mind. I wanted to arrive in the room where I'd be living for months pushing a wheelchair.

When the admissions nurse called our name, my mother and I sat down across from her. She was reading my chart.

"Paralytic polio in 1941?"

I nodded.

"Susan Richards, age eleven. Washington, D.C. 3458 Macomb Street." She looked up from the chart. "Referred by Dr. Something-or-other, I can't read his name, at the Cleveland Clinic. You're here for a stabilization of the right ankle, muscle transplants, et cetera, et cetera. Have you seen Dr. Iler?"

"We haven't," my mother said. "We just arrived last night by car."

"Could you stand up and let me take a look at you?" the nurse asked.

I stood up.

"Walk."

I walked a little way from the desk with the halting kangaroo jump I used for moving back and forth. Out of the corner of my eye I could see Joey Buckley watching me.

"Just for the records," she said.

"What's for the records?" my mother asked.

"That I asked to see her walk. Most of our patients don't walk. Or rarely, they have paralysis in their arms and shoulders and can walk but not manipulate their arms or hands." She gave me a smile, and I'm sure she meant it nicely, but I took her gesture as combative.

"Lucky girl," she said.

"When do I get my own wheelchair?" I asked.

"Your own?" The nurse shook her head. "The wheelchairs you see in the waiting room belong to children who need them at home."

Looking across at me, she must have sensed my longing to be like everybody else.

"Thank your lucky stars," she said in her deep southern drawl, "you don't need a wheelchair."

My mother was always calm, especially in emergencies, and although this wasn't an emergency, I was grateful for the softness of her voice, the absence of general tension, which she concealed with too much success for her own good.

But she knew I was working myself into a state. At some level, she must have known that I didn't want to walk into a place where I'd be living for a long time without having the right equipment.

My mother leaned over the desk, her hand on the top of it, her voice quizzical.

"You seem to have some old wheelchairs lined up against the wall," she said to the nurse.

The nurse's head shot up.

"We do," she said.

"I wonder if we could borrow one."

"For what?" the nurse asked, handing papers to sign across her desk.

"For my daughter," my mother said. She gave no other explanation.

"Your daughter doesn't need a wheelchair," the nurse said, giving my mother a look.

There was a moment of silence while my mother signed the papers and handed them back to the nurse, and then a significant pause. My mother was excellent at silence. We were accustomed to the power of her silence at home.

"She actually does need a wheelchair," my mother said softly.

An orderly brought a large wooden and wicker wheelchair and I sat in it, squiggled into the back of the seat so my legs stuck straight out, and my mother wheeled me over to the chairs where my father sat with Jeffrey talking to Mr. Buckley.

"We're ready," she said to my father.

"Where'd you get the wheelchair?" Joey asked.

"I'm trying it out," I said.

"It's too big for you."

He reached into the corner of his wheelchair and pulled out a baseball cap with ALABAMA in red letters.

"This is the school where I'm going to play ball if I get well," he said. "You can have it if you want."

At Home in Second Medical

I WATCHED MY ROOMMATE tilt her body cast forward so she could eat. I was trying not to talk to her because she had asked me to be quiet, to please be quiet, but I couldn't bear the silence.

"I don't like the grits, do you?" I asked.

"The grits are fine," she said without looking up.

The room was hot and she had nothing on but a sheet thrown over the back of her and a body cast that went from her chest to her feet in a kind of U, so her legs curved up toward her back, and her legs were separated by a pole. She could be turned on her back, but mainly she was on her stomach, sideways across the bed, her elbows resting for support on a metal table. She was in the body cast after surgery on her back, which had been done in the hope that she'd be able to sit up without a back brace.

Her name was Caroline Slover. She was also eleven, and she grew up in a small town in the center of Illinois. She had had polio in fourth grade, when she was nine, and almost died. I knew that from her mother, Mrs. Slover, who delivered the information without emotion, including the part about dying, because Caroline didn't talk about it.

"She'll say nothing about polio, ever," Mrs. Slover said.

We had been living together for three days, and so far I had done all of the talking while Caroline stared out the window or at the wall behind my bed, at a photograph of a field of sunflowers, or read Nancy Drew. She would answer if I asked her a simple impersonal question, and I struggled to think of questions like that to begin a conversation that at least was a facsimile of friendship.

"I don't know what to do," I said to my mother.

"Nothing," my mother said. "Nothing you can do but wait."

Caroline didn't like me. She came to that decision when I first wheeled my oversized wooden and wicker wheelchair into the room I'd be sharing with her and said hi and told her my name. I could feel the animosity like a pop in her corner of the room.

"I can't wait," I told my mother. "I need to fix it right away before you leave."

I had a list of things that needed to be accomplished in the next month before my mother left. In my mind it was simply a list of important things that had nothing to do with the fear of my mother's leaving or the need to establish a stockade of safety around me. If asked, I would have said, "I'm perfectly fine."

I don't think this was a passive way of saying one thing and meaning the opposite. Insofar as I'm able to sort out the child I was from what I know about that child now, I believed at the time that I was capable of dealing with anything that came my way. My mother had told me that.

"Bad things happen to everyone," she'd tell me, recounting the various misfortunes in the lives of people we knew — sinus conditions, the death of parents, automobile accidents, cancer of the voice box, blindness. "You are fine."

Caroline and I were in the room alone, too early in the morning for visitors. My mother was at the hotel with my father and Jeffrey, who had come down with a virus. Caroline's mother was at one of the cottages, which she had rented from the foundation so she could be with Caroline through her surgeries. My mother planned to share the cottage with her for the month she was with me.

"I guess you know I'm having surgery tomorrow morning," I said to Caroline after the nurse had taken our breakfast trays away.

"Everyone has surgery in Second Medical," Caroline said.

I slipped off the bed into the wheelchair I'd be using after the surgery and wheeled over to the door.

What I wanted to do was go down the corridor, past the Girls' Ward, past the nurses' station to the other end of Second Medical, where the boys lived, and find Joey Buckley. But the hall was full of nurses and orderlies and stretchers, and a priest was headed in my direction.

I pulled my wheelchair back inside the door.

Caroline was reading, her blond wavy hair falling across her cheek separating us like a curtain.

I watched her concentrate on her book as if I weren't in the room, as if I didn't exist.

"So there's a priest coming to our room," I said.

But she was deep into Nancy Drew.

I wanted to win her over. I didn't know why it was so important to me, since there was no sign of future friendship from her. Perhaps I was less interested in the friendship than in capturing her attention, but those lines were foggy to me then.

I think about friendship and sometimes wonder even now: Who is this person I bring with me into a room or a conversation or a party, into a friendship? I think of myself as warm and open in ways that I wasn't when I was younger. A loose cannon then, full of energy and determination and unbridled enthusiasm.

But something was missing then and is missing still. It has taken years in this profession of writing, which brings me face to face with my own image, to recognize how much distance I keep between myself and other people. And why?

After my father died, when I was in my twenties, people came back from the funeral to our house, people from every corner of his world, and I was standing at the front door when one of his oldest friends approached and took me aside. I was so glad to see him, so eager to hear what he might say about my father, since so many of the people who came through the door were strangers to me. I imagined that this man would tell me a secret about my father, to keep as a nugget with things I'd missed knowing about him, since he died young. What he said astonished me.

"I just have to tell you now that for thirty years I knew your father." His voice was thick with emotion. "And I hardly knew him."

And twelve years later, at my mother's funeral, sitting at the graveside next to my stepfather, a dear, gentle, military-minded man. He was so different from my father that my brother and I were astounded by her choice.

"I loved your mother," he said, turning to me with tears running down his cheeks. "But I hardly knew her."

Those two stories rest together in my mind as a matched set. I was my parents' daughter.

The priest came in the door, rushing in as if blown by a light wind, tousling Caroline's hair, pulling up the chair at the end of my bed, and sitting down next to my wheelchair.

"I'm on my surgery rounds," he said, "and you're new and having surgery tomorrow, and you just got here on Monday."

He had a wonderful face, angular, of high color, a sharp nose, water-blue eyes, thinning blond hair. A kind, all-around sparkle, as if he'd been sprinkled with glitter. I was breathless in his presence.

"I'm having a stabilization tomorrow," I said. "Do you know that operation?"

"I do, I do. Dr. Irwin will do your stabilization, and he's a genius at this operation. Boom, boom, and it's done. Zip, zip, and you're sewed up. A new cast, a little blood, a little pain, and you're off and running. Right, Caroline?"

They both laughed, and I was surprised that Caroline didn't seem to mind the kind of wild energy this priest brought into the room.

"This is your first visit at Warm Springs, isn't it," he said.

"And maybe it will be my last," I said.

"Maybe so. You never know, but you'll have to come to Mass on

Sundays." He reached over and ran his hand down the side of my cheek. I must have shivered. He had sealed my love for him with that gesture.

"It doesn't matter what religion you are or if you're no religion at all. Just come. It's a pretty ceremony, with incense and wafers and wine and music. And besides, there isn't a lot to do on Sundays at Warm Springs."

He reached into his pocket and took out a tiny book, about the size of a fifty-cent piece, with a brown cover and real pages and writing on the pages that I couldn't read. "This is from Italy. I got it in Florence. Now you have a good-luck piece for tomorrow."

"How did you know I'd be here?" I asked.

"I knew," he said.

Then he got up, stood next to Caroline's bed, leaned on his folded arms, and spoke to her quietly so I couldn't hear what he was saying. But her head was turned toward him and she was smiling.

I put the little book in the pocket of my blouse, aware that I was trembling, a kind of all-over electric tremble. Not like a shiver down my back; more pervasive and unsettling than a shiver.

"So I'll see you some Sunday," he called as he left.

I went to the door and watched him walk down the corridor, stopping in every room.

"Who is that?" I asked Caroline.

"Father James," she said. "He's Catholic."

"Do you go to Mass on Sundays?"

"I'm Protestant," she said, "and I go to nothing."

I added Mass to my mental list.

I loved the ceremony of religion and played it as if it were a game that delighted me in all its permutations. I think my attraction to religion had to do with theater, though I liked the idea of God, not an angry God or even a benevolent one, but a God like the wind, with sufficient force to lift a small girl into the air until she was weightless.

My parents both came from religious families but were nonbelievers with no intention of raising their children in the church in any formal way. My mother described to me the painful hours spent on her knees as a young girl with her Methodist grandfather, and my father grew up with Quakers and Lutherans. He was more Quaker than Lutheran himself, but in general he was nothing at all. When I was very young, I loved Quaker Meeting at Sidwell Friends because the head of the school pretended to have a flea in his ear that represented the Inner Light. At Meeting, when the Inner Light — we never called it God — moved him to speak, he'd take the flea out of his ear and the flea would tell us a story about one thing or another, probably a moral story. That was a long time before Harold Ickes and I remembered those early Meetings as pure magic.

We lived very close to the National Cathedral in Washington, best known for its presidential prayer services and memorial services. The grounds were gorgeously hilly, almost the highest point of the swampy city, with woods and a creek and bridges. There were three Episcopal schools on the property, and playgrounds where I played when I was growing up, a time of relative safety and freedom. I often went to the Bishop's Garden and into the massive cathedral itself, which housed not only the Episcopalians but other religions too.

My particular discovery was the Greek Orthodox church that held services in the crypt of the cathedral. I find it hard to believe now, having raised children in a different time, that I used to wander around the crypt of the cathedral alone. But I did. At about the same time, my mother, who liked the Episcopal Church in the abstract because of its connection to the Church of England, and she liked England, decided I should go to Sunday school at St. Albans Episcopal Church, which was also on the grounds of the cathedral.

I hated the Sunday school, but in no time at all I was skipping it to attend the Greek Orthodox service in the crypt. My parents would leave Jeffrey with Grandma Richards, drop me off at St. Albans, and then head to the diner for breakfast. I would wave goodbye to them, go through the front door of St. Albans, pass the schoolrooms where I was virtually unknown, leave by the back door, and cut across the close to the cathedral. By the time my parents returned from the diner, I was waiting in front of St. Albans where they had let me off. They never asked me how I'd liked Sunday school. I assume they were surprised that I continued to look forward to Sunday mornings, but this secret was one among many of the silences between us.

I was small for my age and traveling alone, but as I remember it no one ever stopped me to ask what I was doing in the cavernous cathedral, descending the precarious winding marble steps into the crypt, stopping at the door to the Greek Orthodox service to light my candles for the dead. I used my money for a St. Albans offering to buy candles for the living — one for my parents, one for Jeffrey, and one for General Beauregard. Sometimes I left out General Beauregard, but more often I left out Grandma Richards, because I didn't have enough money for both and had to choose between them.

I'd stand at the back of the dark church, thick with the scent of incense. At the altar was a screen of thin cloth through which the congregants could see the bearded priest — the very mental picture I had of God, large, cloaked, with a heavy gray beard down to his chest and hair to his shoulders — carrying out the Sunday service. We saw him as a shadow through the screen.

The people at the Greek Orthodox church were very warm and physical with one another and with me, their visiting penitent, in a way I'd never experienced. It was altogether satisfactory. If I had been asked, when I met Father James at Warm Springs, whether I believed in God, I would have said yes, in spite of my parents' feelings about religion. And the God I'd have had in mind would have been some combination of the shadowed priest and the flea who lived in the ear of the principal of Sidwell Friends.

I was ready for Father James's invitation to join the Catholics.

That morning after Father James left, I was sitting on my bed looking at the tiny book from Florence he had given me when the orthopedic medical team, two doctors and an orderly carrying what looked to be a toolbox, entered our room. I thought they were coming to do something with me, since I was scheduled for surgery in the morning. But they had come for Caroline.

They pulled the curtains around her bed and shut the door to the room, but I could see through a space in the curtain what they were doing. They turned Caroline on her back. I hadn't seen her on her back before and it looked painful, the way her legs hung over the side of the bed, bent under, and her head hung over the other side, so that she was contorted in a belly-upward curve. They checked her cast, one doctor running his hands between it and her chest, pushing his arm down to her stomach. The orderly and the other doctor stood with the tools on the side of her bed where her legs dangled.

From where I was sitting I could see Caroline's face, with no expression except the flat one I had been watching all day.

"We're going to tighten the screws here, Caroline," the first doctor said, indicating the metal contraption attached to her legs at either end of the pole. "It's going to hurt."

The doctor began working the plaster with his wrench.

"Tell me when," he said, turning. "Now?" he asked.

Caroline shook her head.

"Now?" He had turned the wrench a little more. "Caroline?"

Her face suddenly hardened as if she'd locked her jaw.

"There," the doctor said. "High pain tolerance, Caroline. It takes a lot of self-control not to scream."

He patted her head.

Then they turned her over on her stomach, spread the sheet over her back, and opened the curtains.

"We'll be seeing you tomorrow morning," the doctor said to me. "I'm Dr. Irwin."

And they were gone.

"That must've really hurt," I said, breathless with admiration.

"No," Caroline replied, her face bone-white. "It didn't hurt."

When I was eighteen, I wrote a novel, never published, called *Wooden and Wicker*, about a girl with mild paralysis who goes to Warm Springs hoping to be accepted as the cripple she is considered in her ordinary world, only to find she's not crippled enough. The book's title refers to the old-fashioned wheelchairs that were in occasional use at Warm Springs during my time there. When I started to write this book, I went in search of the manuscript, hoping to stir my recollections for the place and the people I knew there. I discovered the book among the files of an old friend, and reading it again after almost forty years, which I did before I began this memoir, I was surprised to see that my present memory of what happened and my youthful invention of events were so different. I initially wanted to write this book to make sense of what had happened in the years I lived at Warm Springs, but it's difficult to connect the strings of truth.

So the truth of this story is in the way I see it now.

For example, the novel is of course autobiographical. My memory of how I portrayed the protagonist, before I reread the novel, is as a brave, spirited young girl, idealized to be sure, but realistically portrayed from the point of view of autobiography as a girl responsible for causing a lot of trouble. I didn't expect that I had understood that girl at eighteen, when I was writing the novel, in the way that I understand her now, but the sappy, sentimentalized Victoria of *Wooden and Wicker* is nobody I remember in either fiction or fact. She's a little piece of victimized misery, and I was glad to see her go when I finished reading. Which made me question the character of Caroline Slover, my roommate during the first four months I lived at Warm Springs. The Caroline in *Wooden and Wicker* is a whiner, so I assume that at eighteen I invented these characters out of whole cloth or else my perspective on them, and certainly on myself, has changed. I have never seen or corresponded with any of these people as an adult, except for the Caroline I write about here, and she's a strong and independent woman.

A reason, maybe the real reason, I never made an effort to be in touch with these people, who were so central to me for an important period of my growing up, is part of the reason I wanted to write this book in the first place. Not so much to discover anyone I'd lost, but to understand why I had wanted to lose them.

Patient Number Three

WHEN THE NURSE pushed the stretcher into our room to take me down to surgery, I was wearing the Alabama baseball cap that Joey Buckley had given me. She took off the cap and covered me with a sheet.

"What's going to happen now?" I asked as she pushed the stretcher toward the door.

I looked over at Caroline, who was painting with watercolors in a sketchpad on the metal table by her bed. She had her eye on me with that flat expression she sometimes had.

"Am I going straight to the operating room?" I asked.

"No," Caroline said. "You'll have to wait. We always have to wait."

"You're number three," the nurse said, angling my stretcher through the door. "Number two is in the OR now."

"So where are you taking me?"

My mother had already told me what to expect, but I was hoping to engage this nurse in charge of my immediate future. I wanted eye contact and conversation. I had become expert at achieving both with doctors and nurses and orderlies in the various hospitals I'd been in. I had learned to soften the expression in my eyes so the pupils didn't dilate, to chat in an easygoing way, to ask a nurse about her family, to say I liked her hair or her necklace, her summer tan, something personal and disarming so that she'd devote herself to me for however long we were to be together. I had learned to be winning and funny, to fix a listener in my gaze so he was captured by the intensity of my attention. My life depended on a certain charm.

"Where are your parents?" the nurse asked. "Most parents come with me to the holding room."

There was judgment in her voice, and I didn't want it to fall in my parents' direction.

"I asked them not to see me before surgery," I said.

I had told my parents that I wanted to be alone the morning of my operation weeks before we left Washington for Warm Springs. I knew what I required of myself to rise to the occasion of my parents' fear and sadness.

"Whatever suits you," the nurse said, pushing my stretcher into the elevator, pressing the button for the lower level. "But I feel sorry for *them*."

Later, waiting in the holding room, I wondered about what the operating room nurse had said, wondered whether it was selfish for me to keep my parents at a distance during a time like this, whether I was being self-protective at their expense. I knew above all that I wanted their admiration, and that seemed difficult to earn as a sick child with a reputation for causing trouble.

I had a habit of playing out scenes in advance, a whole scene on the stage set of my brain, and in this particular scene, as I imagined it, I'd be lying on the stretcher, my parents standing on either side, looking down at me with such sorrowful expressions I couldn't take on the responsibility for them.

We had a small family — two children, one dog, one grandmother, two parents — and we lived far away from the town where my parents had grown up. We were a typical postwar nuclear family, sufficient unto itself and in retrospect very lonely. My parents had traded the narrow life of a midwestern town for the independent isolation of the urban East Coast, and there was about us a kind of pride in that. But I think, especially on my father's part, there was shame as well. He had escaped from the provinces to forge his own life and had been punished for this breach with a damaged child. Whether he believed this or not, I can only guess. God knows we never spoke of it. But I had overheard or been told stories that led me to a certain kind of thinking about the sacrifices my parents had made. I knew, for example, that my father had given up a job in Europe during the war because I was ill. I knew this because my mother told me that she worried over the short shrift she gave to my compliant little brother in favor of me. I knew my father missed my mother's company.

The elevator doors opened on the first-floor corridor in front of the waiting room. At one end of the corridor was the operating room, and we turned in that direction, passing the waiting room. As the nurse wheeled my stretcher down the corridor, I caught sight of my parents looking out the window toward the courtyard. My father's hands were behind his back, holding one of my mother's hands in his. My mother was in a dusty-rose linen dress, looking young and strong in that fleeting image. I turned my head away.

The nurse took me into the small, windowless room where patients were taken to wait their turn for surgery. The room was empty except for a hard-backed chair and an iron lung, and she pushed my stretcher alongside it, so close I could touch the metal cylinder.

"Who else is having surgery today?" I asked.

"Four of you. I don't remember the names."

I gave her my name so she'd remember it and told her I was from Washington, D.C. I added that I had a boyfriend named Harold Ickes, whose father had worked in the White House with President Roosevelt. It was my effort to establish a personal connection to Roosevelt, but she didn't show an interest.

"Did I tell you I was going to give you something to make you sleepy?" she asked.

There must have been something like valium in the enema she gave me, and it felt as if bubbly water in the colors of the rainbow or shooting stars were flying through my blood.

"That's it," she said. "You're done. When I come back you'll be asleep, and when I take you to the operating room, you'll get put out completely so you won't feel a thing."

"And then what?" I called to her.

But she had gone out the door.

The iron lung was a long green coffin, and in my fuzzy-minded, drugged state I was drawn to look at it, at the pillow on the end of the bed inside it, where the patient's head would be, his body immobilized in the metal contraption. I'd seen a little girl in an iron lung at the Cleveland Clinic, her curly yellow hair spread on the pillow, and I'd been fascinated by the *whoosh whoosh* of the machine as the air went in and out.

I'd said hello as I passed her, and she'd smiled at me with her glazed eyes.

Her name was Sally, the doctor said while he examined me, and she had died the day after I saw her, he told me later.

"Did she die because of the iron lung?" I asked him.

"She died of polio," he said.

She was perhaps the first person I had seen who was actually sick with the poliomyelitis virus, and for years I couldn't get rid of the image of her flushed cherubic face and yellow curls and the grip of her eyes as she tried to engage me.

I didn't remember anything about my own polio, although I was told that I had been paralyzed, that the paralysis had lasted a few weeks, and that I had screamed in pain whenever someone got close. But to me it was as though I'd been born with a crippled leg. I didn't know how it felt to walk normally, so the trauma of paralysis was not a conscious memory. In absolute terms, I didn't know what it was like to have paralytic polio, although I knew what it meant to be trapped in bed.

Polio is an old virus. We have evidence from the ancient world of polio-like deformities, and later, in the Middle Ages, there are references to paralyzed children. Clusters of epidemics were reported by physicians in the nineteenth century. A rural community in Louisiana, for example, had a number of serious cases that occurred over a period of time suggesting an epidemic. The first recorded outbreak in the United States happened in 1894, near Rutland, Vermont, where a young country doctor interested in public health kept a record that revealed that the majority of cases were male and under six years of age, and that the symptoms were headache, nausea, fever, fatigue, and stiff neck.

A public record indicating, as this did, that polio was contagious suggested the possibility of widespread epidemics.

In June 1916 there was an epidemic in a part of Brooklyn known as Pigtown, populated by recent Italian immigrants, and the rapid spread of polio there was attributed to filthy conditions. The new immigrants were blamed as the carriers of infectious disease. As a result, Pigtown was isolated and cleaned up by the New York City Board of Health with the usual methods of disease control: quarantine and sanitation. But the epidemic had spread, continuing for months, eventually resulting in twenty-seven thousand deaths across America.

Those who studied the outbreak were concerned that the measures taken had not controlled the spread of the disease. Wealthy neighborhoods and rural areas were as affected as squalid urban centers. In fact, it appeared that a child living in poverty might even be protected from the virus by frequent exposure and a more developed immune system.

In the twentieth century, Americans became obsessed with cleanliness. Protection against viral-borne diseases like polio consisted of soap and water, frequent baths and hand washing, clean sheets and clothes, clean toilets and kitchens and public facilities.

In the case of polio, however, the result of the anti-germ revolution was, ironically, more frequent outbreaks of the disease.

In 1941, when I had polio, it was generally known that the disease was not associated with filth, but myths persisted about swimming in public pools, playing in sandboxes in public playgrounds, and summer heat as breeders of the disease. Mothers like mine still associated polio with scummy conditions and poverty. For years, my mother would defend the protective measures she took against germs.

"I even sterilized the orange before I made your orange juice," she'd say.

In the early 1950s, the National Foundation for Infantile Paralysis, established by President Roosevelt and headed by his law partner Basil O'Connor, was funding the research of several scientists, including Jonas Salk at the University of Pittsburgh, whose lab was developing a vaccine for polio. Salk grew all three of the identified viruses, testing them on tissue from the kidneys of monkeys. He then fed the viruses with a solution called Mixture 1999 so they multiplied. Finally he killed the viruses with a formaldehyde solution and created the vaccine by combining the three strains of dead viruses. At the same time, another scientist, Albert Sabin, believed that the only vaccine that would succeed in developing immunity was one made from live polio viruses. There was a competitive "race for the cure" between Salk and Sabin, which was the background music for the two years I was living at Warm Springs.

The iron lung in the holding room in which I waited operated like a bellows. Once a patient was enclosed in the machine, a perfect seal was created. A patient with bulbar polio couldn't use his breathing muscles to inflate the lungs, so air was pumped out of the casing, causing a reduction in pressure that forced the patient's chest to rise, filling the lungs with air flowing through the nose and mouth. When the air was allowed back in, the pressure increased, forcing the lungs to empty. Thus the operating principle of bellows.

An active iron lung is frightening — the body concealed, the head exposed, air whooshing in and out. But at least the living patient is present.

An empty iron lung looks like death.

I was in a coma for a couple of weeks when I had spinal menin-gitis. I still have recollections of hearing voices during that time I spent in isolation. I heard them as if at a great distance, and I couldn't take hold of them beyond the background din of sound, so I couldn't make out what it was they were saying. Dr. Nichol-son was at the hospital with me and stayed, off and on, for those weeks, sometimes through the night, so I wouldn't be afraid if I regained consciousness.

My mother was told she couldn't come into the isolation ward. Instead, she wandered the streets of downtown Washington, fill-ing the tin cups of the beggars who sat with their monkeys and their boxes of change, their harmonicas and their foul language. And then, as she later told me, she would go home to her new baby and wait for Dr. Nicholson's report.

I remember thinking that one of the voices I heard in the dis-tance was my mother's and wondering whether I was dead. I asked her later, after I recovered, if that was what death sounded like. I knew death was possible. Children in the meningitis isola-tion ward had died when I was there.

As a child, I thought a lot about death. The key, as I saw it, was not to fall asleep.

At the farm where we lived after I got out of the hospital, where my parents had moved in order to protect us from the city, from disease and other dangers, I could not sleep at night.

I had a puppy called Trixie, one of the farm dogs, given to me when I got home from the hospital, who slept on my bed, and outside my window I could see the barn and the chicken coop and the pig shed. Jeffrey slept in the bedroom next to mine in his bas-sinet, and next to that was my parents' room. I loved the sounds of the farm and the brightness of the stars at night, yet with all that company in close and safe proximity I couldn't fall asleep.

So I would make a list of the things that frightened me, and af-ter my light was out, my father, always my father, who was the worldly force, would come to the door of my room to hear my litany of fears.

Promise not poison, I'd say.

Promise no snakes under my bed.

Promise no rats in the wall.

Promise no thunder.

Promise no bedbugs.

Promise I won't die.

He would promise me each of these impossibles one by one, never impatient, never complaining.

Even my logical, fair-minded mother would make these promises she knew she could not keep, when my father was traveling or stuck in Washington, not enough gas to get home to Vienna because of wartime rationing. I'd ask her for promises and she would repeat after me: "Promise not poison. Promise no snakes. Promise no rats in the wall."

A couple of years later, when we moved to the house in Cleveland Park, I told my father that I'd stop the Promise Problem, one promise at a time. But I couldn't, and the ritual went on and on, until one night when I was about seven, my father said, "This is the last night for promises."

And it was over.

I must have been relieved to end this desperate charade. And the raw fear at the source of these promises dropped somewhere out of sight, to a place I didn't know was there, but could at any moment expand and rise like an air balloon.

Fading from the effects of my psychedelic enema, the iron lung within easy reach, I kept my eyes wide open so I wouldn't fall asleep.

"It's not taking, Dr. Iler," I heard a nurse say just outside my room. "She's still awake."

"Give her another enema," he said. "She'll go out like a light."

The nurse came in and slid between my stretcher and the iron lung.

"You didn't do what I asked you to do," she said crossly. "Now I have to give you another enema."

And between the start and the end of it, I was out.

By the time I arrived at Warm Springs, the hospital had a staff of orthopedic surgeons who routinely performed stabilizations to solidify a bone at a joint, like the ankle, since the muscles were insufficient to support the skeleton. They were doing transplants of muscles from one part of the body to another, and very delicate back surgery such as Caroline Slover had had, and leg surgery and hand surgery. A stabilized bone is more dependable than one with joints if the muscles are weak. The surgeons performed many ankle stabilizations like the one I had, in which the ankle is broken and fused, and bone tissue from another part of the body, such as the hip, is grafted onto the ankle bone to strengthen the fused joint. In the case of transplants, some muscles are more essential to walking than others. In my case, I had traces of muscle at the ankle in the front of my leg but no muscle traces remaining in the calf. The muscle from the front was transplanted to the calf, which allowed me to learn to walk from heel to toe. I have no side-to-side movement in the ankle and limited but sufficient movement up and down. These operations were performed with varying degrees of success, but many patients left the hospital with much greater mobility than when they came.

I was a Warm Springs success story, in part because I wasn't severely handicapped and in part, I believe, because my mother had insisted on hours of physical therapy that she did herself. What muscles could be saved from atrophy were saved. The bones in my foot — which looked like a claw bent nearly in half from walking on the beach in Florida after polio, without the muscle strength to protect the bones — were broken and fused. I walked by swinging my hips and using my leg as a peg, and I fell frequently, tripping myself up even with crutches.

In this particular surgery, the doctors broke the bones in my foot to re-form it as a straight, flat foot. It is still crippled, but flat enough to serve as a base for walking. The stabilization was a common operation. The re-forming of the foot was not, since most polios have dropped foot, so the foot hangs down but is not crippled.

On the third day after my surgery, my mother moved into the cottage with Caroline's mother, Mrs. Slover, and by the time my father and Jeffrey left for the drive back to Washington, I was sitting up in bed.

I kissed my father goodbye and watched him walk out holding my somber little brother's hand, my mother's arm around Jeffrey's shoulder. And I think now what a sad sight that was. My poor brother must have felt he was walking off the earth. He didn't know my father well then and was uncomfortable around him and a little afraid. He didn't want to go to first grade without my mother there. He didn't want to leave my mother at all.

None of those thoughts were on my mind that afternoon, and I came to understand only much later what the cost of that separation must have been for Jeffrey, how fractured he felt. But that's retrospective and had nothing to do with the thrill I felt at having my mother to myself.

II

....

What Becomes
an Ordinary Life

Negotiating Safety

I WAS ALONE.

At night before lights out I'd write a list in my Survival Notebook of my plans for the following day, and then I'd read the book of catechism Father James had given me to prepare for my conversion to Roman Catholicism, which I kept inside my latest Nancy Drew mystery. I associated Catholicism with sin and hid the catechism inside Nancy Drew so no one could see what I was reading. I understand now that the association with Catholicism was really sex, not sin, but it's no wonder that at eleven I was confused.

My mother had left Warm Springs the day after Halloween. She might have stayed longer if Jeffrey were not refusing to attend first grade at John Eaton Elementary and if Grandma Richards, under pressure from a six-year-old who threw up every day in the classroom, had not been driven to drink a couple of extra bourbons before dinner. My father was then vice president of the National Association of Broadcasters and spent about eight months of the year traveling. The principal at John Eaton told Grandma Richards that Jeffrey had to be kept at home until either he stopped getting sick or his mother returned. So my mother had no choice but to go home. I don't think it occurred to her to bring Jeffrey to Warm Springs and send him to the public grammar school nearby, although later she wished she had done just that. It's what the parents of my sixties rule-breaking generation might have done, but the mothers of the fifties tended to live by the book — as if school could in any way replace her absence. For all my mother's extraordinary maternal instincts, she was bewildered by boys, tougher with me than she was with Jeffrey, more uncertain with him, more tentative, and less present.

It may have had something to do with the fraught relationship of mothers and daughters. My daughters tell me that I was much easier on my sons. It may have had to do with guilt, but I also know now that the doctors at Warm Springs encouraged parents to leave their children in the hospital's care in order to avoid parental interference with painful treatments. In the end, however, my mother realized that Jeffrey would have been happier living with her in Warm Springs, in or out of school, than at home with General Beauregard and Grandma Richards and, occasionally, my father.

"I'm fine," I told her when she said she had to go home. "I love it here. Don't worry."

Perhaps she believed me. I'm sure she wanted to believe me.

Perhaps I felt the hollow crush of homesickness, the rise of tears, but I don't remember it, and if I did feel homesick, I would not have been inclined to show it.

Halloween had been a failure. Even without the benefit of rereading my unpublished autobiographical novel, in which the insipid heroine hates her roommate for usurping all the prizes, I would remember my first Halloween at Warm Springs.

One of Franklin Roosevelt's goals when he transformed Warm Springs from a decaying spa hotel to a rehabilitation hospital was to create the sense of a normal life so the polio could develop confidence in himself as an ordinary citizen in a place where he felt the safety of home. Physical improvement came second to social adjustment, a concept revolutionary for medicine in the late 1920s, when Roosevelt was the architect, in fact and in spirit, of Warm Springs.

And it worked. There was a generous democratic spirit of fun and even joy when holidays approached, with weeks of planning and anticipation and fanfare. Halloween was the first of many of these during the time I was at Warm Springs. The hospital was electric with excitement as patients put together their costumes. You could feel it in the corridors. Everyone dressed up for the parade around the grounds on a fall day that in Georgia was usually warm and sunny. There were bags of sweets and cotton candy and popcorn and soda and balloons, but the highlight of the occasion was the awarding of prizes.

I was Sunbonnet Sue. My mother's childlike imagination had led to the design of a wheelchair-turned-surrey with Sunbonnet Sue sitting in it, dressed in a calico puff-sleeved dress that covered my legs and a straw bonnet decorated in ribbons, attached to which were construction-paper black-eyed Susans.

It took her weeks to make it all. She'd sit sewing in my room, on the lawn while I sat beside her, in the cottage she shared with Caroline's mother. It was a delicious time together. We'd have milk and cookies or chocolate pie, and she'd tell me stories and I'd tell her stories. We talked and talked and I can't even remember what we talked about, but I know our conversation made the world a place of endless possibilities. I was never bored. She delighted in everything I said, and I loved to watch her pretty hands, such small hands, the way they flew over the material.

Sunbonnet Sue was not my choice of identity. I would have preferred a male figure, someone in jeans and a cowboy hat or bandanna or baseball cap, a boyish character who happened to be in a wheelchair for a reason. He'd been in the war or shot accidentally or attacked in the woods by a wild animal. A character with a dangerous story.

But that character wouldn't have suited my mother at all, would have left her with nothing to do, no role to play in my future success. I was not an ideal dress-up doll for my mother, with my straight dark hair and bony limbs and angular face and damaged leg, so I was happy to sacrifice my vision of myself that Halloween and the chance we had together to win the gold.

Caroline Slover was dressed as a ghost in a ghost car. She had a sheet over her head with holes cut out for the eyes and mouth, and a steering wheel on the front of her stretcher, which her mother had rigged with the help of one of the orderlies. A white blanket was draped over her body and the stretcher, and big cardboard wheels were attached to the blanket to serve as the wheels of the ghost car.

"No one can see who I am," she said, and that pleased her.

I hoped that Caroline would come in second or third in one of the categories, maybe for Best Costume, because she deserved it — not for her costume but for her struggle.

I was sure I would come in first in at least one category. Certainly Originality. Maybe Best in Show.

By inclination I was unsurprised by failure, and good at it, and even felt a kind of satisfaction in the resilience required to bounce back, as if the failure itself were lengthening my chances of survival. But I also always expected to win, and the two were strangely complementary in my mind.

I'm a backstage girl, comfortable there. It's a family trait that each generation tries and fails to overcome. But I'm always imagining that one night the curtains will open and I will be the one onstage.

That Halloween, my confidence in winning had to do with my mother, who was a perfectionist. If she tried something, she succeeded at it.

Caroline Slover won first prize for Originality and came in third for Best in Show.

Everyone got a prize. I came in fourth for Originality.

In the bathroom, where I went as soon as the judging was over, I wept for my mother.

That night, after she had told me goodbye, since she was leaving for Washington early in the morning, I thought about why I had lost — how could I possibly have let her down? And I decided it must have been because I didn't *need* to win. I wasn't sick enough to be awarded first prize, and so I didn't earn it.

At dinner with my mother at the cottage she shared with Caroline's mother, we didn't talk about the prizes.

"It was such fun," she said cheerily. "I loved making your costume and all the time we got to spend together."

"Me too," I said. "The costume was perfect."

We smiled and laughed and she gave me a sip of her wine, and I didn't tell her what I really felt and she didn't tell me what she really felt, and yet we had talked and talked for days, and would again and again in the years ahead, until she died.

Sometime between my arrival at Warm Springs when I was eleven and my departure for the last time when I was almost thirteen, I learned to deal with a small brushfire by starting larger ones all around it, so the troubling small fire would disappear in the conflagration.

On the day my mother left, I met Magnolia. She was sitting under a table in the supply closet where the cleaning supplies, brooms, brushes, mops, and dustpans were kept, stretching a piece of bubblegum so it made a loop from her mouth to her outstretched arm.

I caught her eye and she gave me a big smile. The bubblegum fell out of her mouth, and she made a noise I'd never heard before. It seemed to come out of a hollow in her stomach and reverberate.

I stopped my wheelchair at the closet door and told her hi, but even before I got the word out of my mouth, I felt a great force behind me, and one of the cleaning staff pushed me aside and swooped Magnolia up, knocking her head on the underside of the table, bubblegum all over her fingers and shirt and face.

"I told you not to make a sound," the woman said, setting her down on the table. "You come to work with me and you stay under that table 'til I come get you. Understand me?"

She took Magnolia's face in her hands, put her own face right on the little girl's, and mouthed *no* without making a sound.

I hadn't moved, so when the woman turned her head to find me still sitting where I'd been watching her, her eyes grew dark and fierce.

"Where are you supposed to be living, out and about like you are?" she asked.

"I was going to see if the little girl wanted to play," I said.

"Well, she doesn't want to play," the woman said, but the little girl was smiling a bubblegum smile at me and I smiled back.

"So you get on your way," the woman said.

I turned my wheelchair around and headed down the corridor toward the Boys' Ward, where I wasn't allowed to go. I had seen Joey Buckley only twice since we'd been admitted, once at the movie theater and again when he was leaving the brace shop. I had stopped the second time to talk to him, but an orderly had said they were in a hurry.

"I'm having surgery next week," Joey had called as the orderly pushed his chair toward the Boys' Ward. "Then I'll get to ride in my wheelchair and we can do stuff together."

So he had probably had the surgery and was recovering, I thought. I went all the way down to the end of the corridor, slowing down as I came to the Boys' Ward. I had never been this close before. As long as my mother had been at Warm Springs, I hadn't broken the rules.

A young nurse came clicking out of the ward with a tray of medicines and gave me a look but went on her way. After she was out of sight, I wheeled closer, right up to the door. I could see two beds facing the courtyard and one right next to the door. I didn't have a view of the others.

A boy about my age with carrot-red hair approached from deep inside the ward, walking slowly on crutches with two long leg braces.

"Hi," I said when he came into view.

"Want to come in?" he asked.

"Sure." I wheeled in closer.

"You're not allowed, you know. Some of the guys are on the bedpan now, so they might not be overjoyed to see you."

I pulled back into the corridor, but I didn't leave.

The first bed overlooking the courtyard was empty and unmade. In the second, a boy was lying on his back, an IV in his arm, the foot of the bed elevated and both his legs in casts. I couldn't see his face, but from that distance I could see his head and black hair, and I thought with hair that black, it might be Joey Buckley.

The boy on crutches was talking to the boy in the bed next to the door, and I tried to get his attention.

"Is that Joey Buckley?" I asked, pointing to the boy with the IV.

"It used to be," he replied. "Now it's a sickie with a fever and his operation may have failed. Why do you want to know?"

"He's a friend of mine," I said.

"Yeah? Well, he's a friend of mine too, and he never mentioned your name."

"My name is Susan Richards," I said.

"That's what I mean. I never heard of Susan Richards."

"So what's the matter with him?" I asked.

"You didn't ask my name, so why should I bother to tell you?" the boy said, initiating what would pass for flirting at Warm Springs.

"What *is* your name?" I asked.

"I'm Bruce, but guys call me Leadfoot, for obvious reasons."

He came closer to the door, put his crutches against the bed, and stood with his arms folded across his chest. "Neat, don't you think? I never could stand like this when I came to this hole, and now — bonanza. I'm practically ready for the track team."

I found out that Joey had had surgery the day before, but for some reason the stabilization on one foot had developed an infection, and the doctors were worried.

"Blood poisoning is what they think," Leadfoot said, pointing down the hall, where four doctors were headed in our direction along with a couple of nurses. "And they're taking him out of the ward to a private room."

I didn't have time to get out of the way before the doctors were in my path, and one of the nurses with them took hold of the back of my chair and wheeled me toward the Girls' Ward.

"What is your name?" she asked.

I told her.

"I'm sure you know that you are not permitted in the Boys' Ward."

"I wasn't *in* the Boys' Ward."

"Anywhere *near* the Boys' Ward, Miss Richards," she said.

She left me next to the nurses' station, and I pretended to read a nearby bulletin board while I kept one eye on the activity in the Boys' Ward.

With a nurse holding on to the IV, the doctors pushed Joey's bed into the corridor and turned left down another corridor, where I had never been before. I watched until they disappeared.

"What are you looking at?"

It was Miss Riley, the day nurse, who sat at the desk, sometimes flossing her teeth, sometimes putting her feet up on the desk and napping.

"They're taking a boy out of the Boys' Ward because he has blood poisoning," I said.

"Where did you hear that?"

"Someone told me."

"They're taking him to Second East, but they don't *know* that he has blood poisoning, so you can tell that someone he's probably wrong."

"Okay," I said.

"And Susan," she went on. "I've got my eye on you. The Boys' Ward is off-limits."

The woman from the cleaning staff was picking the bubblegum off the little girl's face when I rode by. I stopped and asked if I could help her or read the little girl a book.

She cocked her head and looked at me.

"She can't hear," she said. "No good reading her a book."

I pushed my wheelchair to the threshold of the closet.

"I could help you," I said. "I'm good at getting bubblegum off faces."

The woman stopped, folded her arms across her chest, and leaned against the table.

"What is your name?"

I told her.

"Well, I don't know where you come from, but in Georgia little white girls don't play with little colored girls, so I don't need your help, you understand?"

The cleaning woman's name was Gertrude. She was from Warm Springs and had been on the cleaning crew of the hospital since she was fifteen. Magnolia was her daughter. She was seven, and deaf, and couldn't go to school because the school didn't accept deaf children, so her mother took Magnolia to work and put her under the table in the closet so she wouldn't bother anybody with the noises she made in her effort to communicate.

I have always been good at getting people to tell me things, and by the end of our conversation I knew a lot about Gertrude, including the fact that I wouldn't be able to play with Magnolia because I was white and the other people in the hospital would see to it that Gertrude was fired if a white girl was found playing with her deaf and colored daughter.

I sat on my bed in the room I shared with Caroline and told her what had happened, and she told me the truth as she saw it.

"You get in people's business," she said. "And why do you do that?"

She had a way with people that must have come from her no-nonsense parents and the small Illinois town where she'd grown up, probably in a Protestant churchgoing family. She had a tendency to be didactic, judgmental, and she didn't try to soften her observations with flattery. I was a likely candidate for her consideration — provocative, stubborn, a little foolhardy, and curious to the point of stupidity.

I had come to admire Caroline, even to like her. We would never be good friends, in the sense of real girlfriends, but I wasn't necessarily cut out for that kind of friendship. I was by instinct and circumstance an outsider. And Caroline was a good girl, the kind of girl she had probably been before polio, but afterward it was her trump card, what my mother used to call true blue.

"I don't *mean* to get in people's business," I said.

I must have known that was a lie even as I was saying it, and certainly Caroline knew it.

"So what are you planning to do about Magnolia?" she asked. "Play with her anyway?"

"She'd like for me to play with her."

"Something bad is sure to happen if you do." She shrugged, a familiar expression on her face, not of criticism so much as warning.

"It doesn't make sense that we can't play together, does it?" I asked. "Does it make sense to you?"

"It's the way it is." She looked over at me with her eyes half closed, as if this conversation had already gone on too long.

It made me mad. As if Caroline were thirty-five and I were some dim-witted child.

"I don't think you know very much about the troubles of colored people," I said.

"I don't," she said.

When we moved to the farm in Vienna, Virginia, in December of 1944, I was just recovering from meningitis and Jeffrey was six weeks old. The farm had an old house with about fifteen acres of land, which my parents had bought for ten thousand dollars. There were a couple of tenant cottages on the property, housing two black families: Mary and John Cash, and Mary's sister Aida, Aida's husband Guy, and their children. These families became our built-in social life and, as it turned out, my father's first real introduction to race in the South. He'd come home at night from Washington, head over to Guy's house after dinner, and play cards and drink beer and tell stories, perhaps feeling he was replicating the evenings of his childhood. My father had grown up in poverty in an Underground Railroad town in Ohio, where the social divisions were economic, not racial; he lived in a black neighborhood literally on the other side of the railroad tracks from most of the white families.

I remember the farm in high relief. I thought it the most beautiful place on earth, smelling of sugar cookies and newborn puppies, the radio playing in the kitchen, my mother holding me and dancing with Mary Cash, Jeffrey making baby sounds in his carriage. I loved the kitchen, where something was always cooking.

If there was rising tension on the farm, I didn't notice it. But my parents, especially my father, must have been aware of some discomfort developing between the black families and them. My father had become a regular at the houses out back, crossing the boundaries of race and class with which the black families on the farm were familiar. They came to our house for dinner from time to time but refused to eat in the dining room, preferring to stand in the kitchen, dishing up their meal from the pots on the stove as if they were hired hands and not guests.

On the Fourth of July that year, my father and Guy and John Cash butchered a pig and hung the carcass upside down by a big hook, the blood draining out on the floor of the shed that was attached to the kitchen. Why they butchered so early in the summer, I don't know. And why they shot the pig with a shotgun — not the common way to butcher — I don't know either. There are so many questions I never asked, never thought to ask, until there was no one left to answer. But the butchering did leave a couple of loaded shotguns around our house and theirs, in easy reach for the Fourth of July celebrations.

That night, John and Guy and some friends were playing cards at Guy's house and got drunk and started shooting their shotguns in the air. Somehow, someone shot Aida and Aida's daughter, superficial wounds that bled a lot. The women, seeking safety, brought the children over to our house, and my mother took them in.

I was under the kitchen table, more thrilled than afraid to be a part of this high drama. My mother was, always was, preternaturally calm. That night she was wearing a white sundress, and I thought she was brave and lovely, standing barefoot, her white dress striped red with blood, her arms around the women.

The men, by then quite drunk and boisterous, came up to the house and shouted at my father that if he didn't let the women and children go, they were going to kill him.

My father, who was guarding the back door, asked my mother to call the police, who told her to handle the problem herself. They refused to intervene in a family struggle involving race, they said, and told my mother that she had been foolish to take the women in, that what she should do was open the door, turn the women out, and lock the door behind them.

All night I sat with my parents in their double bed, from where we could see the tenant houses, and watched the men set off fireworks in the Cashes' front yard.

The following day, my parents put the farm on the market and we moved back to the city.

For my father, the incident was a failure of understanding, his failure, but it didn't stop him from trying again. By the time I was seven we were living in segregated Washington with a college-educated black woman who could not get a civil service job because of Negro quotas and the fact that she was a single mother of two children. She worked for my parents, but at their insistence an illusion of equality prevailed. It would be dishonest to say that we were not separated by class and color, because we were. But I was young, and my perception of the world of race was influenced by my father's romanticism and my childhood history of proximity and comfort. The idea that I wasn't allowed to play with a little black girl because her mother might be fired for it was a challenge.

Magnolia was lying on her stomach under the table in the cleaning closet several days later when I wheeled down the corridor in search of news about Joey Buckley. She made a sound and I turned and she smiled at me, crawling out from under the table over to my wheelchair. I picked her up and set her on my lap and wheeled down the corridor past the nurses' station, where Miss Riley looked up and smiled. Miss Riley actually smiled at me, as I told Gertrude later, so I punched the down arrow on the elevator and headed to the Children's Ward with Magnolia.

It made me blissfully happy to ride into the ward with Magnolia on my lap, her skinny arm wrapped around my neck, and if the nurses in the ward were disturbed by it, they didn't show it.

The Children's Ward

I HAD MADE A LIFE in the Children's Ward even before my mother returned to Washington to take care of Jeffie.

"He's not happy in school, but he's happy that I'm back," she wrote in one of her letters about daily life on Macomb Street.

I kept her letters in a little purse, like a passport case, that my mother had made for me years before which I could hang around my neck; it had a list of emergency telephone numbers in case something happened to me. The letters from my mother were short but frequent and sometimes funny, like the one she wrote after she got home:

> Grandma Richards has traded in the extra bourbon for sa-shaying past Granfer Swindells's house although Granfer isn't interested in dating Grandma R. in spite of the crino-line skirts she wears under her dresses and the nice rubbery boobs she purchased at G. C. Murphy's.
> P.S. I hope you're having fun with the babies.

On weekdays in October, my mother would take a break from designing my Sunbonnet Sue costume to come with me to the Children's Ward, so I'd be permitted to go in with the babies by myself after she left.

That first fall, we went to the Children's Ward for short visits, my mother wandering after me while I went from bed to bed. She made friends with one of the nurses, a tiny, round, red-faced blonde with a tight permanent like yellow Slinkys all over her head and a crooked smile. Miss Browning, I called her, and after my mother went home, she told me I could call her Paisley Jean if she was the only nurse on duty, but Miss Browning if one of the other "broads" was there. She called women "broads" and men "barn rats" and the babies "my precious ones," and I liked her better than any of the other nurses at Warm Springs, who tended to be strict about rules.

I called the ward the Babies' Ward. Just the word "babies," repeated in my head, had a visceral effect, as if my body warmed to the sound of the double *b*'s spoken in my own voice. There were ten babies when I first arrived in late August, but one of them, Belly Boo — I called her Belly Boo because she was round in the middle and very quiet but I could make her smile by playing peekaboo — left to go home to Nebraska, a limp little Raggedy Ann with floppy legs and a circle of curly red hair at the very top of her head.

I loved all those babies, with their silky skin and red-hot cheeks from the endless summer heat pressing into autumn. I'd take one out of her crib onto my lap and she'd wrap her tiny arms around my neck and look at me with a trust and adoration I had never known, and I'd fill up as if the soft summer air were stretching my skin until it became something more than simply skin.

I'd move from crib to crib, gentling them one after the other, telling them stories, taking them in my lap for a wheelchair ride.

Magnolia made her hollow, grunting noises when we went through the door into the ward, and the babies had their eyes on me as they always did when I arrived, pulling themselves up by the bars of the cribs or lying on their backs, waiting for me to lean over their beds, lift them out, and set them on my lap. I could tell they didn't like the sounds coming out of Magnolia, so I put a finger to my lips and then to hers and she went silent.

Paisley Jean was in a rocking chair with Rosie, rocking her to sleep, and the only other nurse in the ward had left after I arrived.

We stopped at Little Maria's crib first.

Little Maria looked Spanish, maybe Latin American, and she

could walk by holding on to the side of the crib. She would lean against the railing and stretch out her arms for me to pick her up.

"This is Little Maria," I said, putting her on my lap next to Magnolia. "She's going home next month to Chicago to see her big brother and her daddy."

Magnolia turned her head away.

She couldn't read lips, but she looked at me when I was speaking, and I talked to her as if she could hear.

"Watch this," I said to Magnolia.

I played a finger game with Little Maria, a ritual I had begun by playing the same game every day with each child, changing the game depending on the child, so I was *someone* to each of them. No one could take my place.

"Want to play church?" I asked Little Maria, and she clapped her hands.

I'd make a church with my fingers folded in.

"Here's the church and here's the steeple," I said while she tried to put her hands together like mine.

I opened my thumbs, turned my hands palm-down so the woven fingers showed.

"Open the door and see all the people!"

And Little Maria fell over backward with squeals of laughter, giggling until I lifted her into her crib and she cried out to me, "Mamamamama."

I loved that.

"I promise I'll be back tomorrow," I said to Little Maria.

I kept my promises with the babies.

I wasn't permitted to pick up Sue Sue because she was too fragile. She lay on her back, her head turned in my direction, her eyes glazed, a tiny smile on her face.

I pulled my wheelchair right next to her bed, lowered my voice, and whispered the story I told her every day, the same one each morning.

"Once upon a time there was a very small rabbit with a pink

nose and long whiskers and one eye," I began, speaking through the bars.

I'd finish the one-eyed-rabbit story and then I'd reach through the bars and run my fingers very lightly over Sue Sue's cheeks, the way my mother did with me before I went to sleep at night.

Violet Blue was lying on her side, pale-skinned with straight black hair and bangs.

I don't know where I got the name Violet Blue, but it came to me the first time I saw her. She was the only child in the ward who was not a baby — two years old and paralyzed below the waist, with large, oval, olive-colored eyes flecked yellow and a violent temper.

What I especially loved about Violet Blue was her temper and the way I could make it disappear.

This morning, with Magnolia still in my lap but getting restless, Violet Blue was sitting up, supported by the crib rails behind her, hammering her little fists against the mattress. She didn't stop when she saw me approach, and as I drove my wheelchair up beside the crib, she threw herself backward, hitting the top of her head, screaming bloody murder.

Magnolia was fascinated. She climbed out of my lap, wrapped her fingers around the metal rails of the crib, and pressed her face against them.

Usually a nurse would come by and lift Violet Blue into my lap, since I couldn't pick her up without help, but this time only Paisley Jean was left, and she was rocking Rosie, my beloved Rosie, the ultimate object of my adoration. I loved each of the babies, but I loved Rosie best.

Magnolia squished her face against the rails.

Violet Blue lay perfectly still, watching her.

Magnolia must have been uneasy with such scrutiny, a little girl used to being left alone under some desk or table looking out at the world. She began to make low growls, which soon became a roar.

Violet Blue reached out and took hold of the railing, her fat little fingers wound around it. She pulled her limp body along and sat very close to Magnolia, both hands gripping the railing, unsmiling, looking at the deaf child with what might have been hostility. It was something close to anger in any case, and I must have known then that trouble was about to happen.

On a typical day — and most days at Warm Springs were the same, different only in what a child made of them, and mainly in her head — I'd arrive at the Children's Ward in the morning, after breakfast. I'd drive my wheelchair through the double doors as if it were a convertible with the top down, my hair flying, the wind stinging my cheeks, racing to my babies. That was what I pretended.

I was in charge of the Babies' Ward, the one person in the hospital responsible for this gathering of innocence. Without me, these orphan wonders, terrorized by the nurses and doctors, would fold themselves into the corner of their cribs and die.

I was their life, that was how I imagined it, and for those few hours every day when I was allowed to take the babies, one at a time, out of their cribs, take them anywhere around the hospital except the wing for the sick patients, I was a heroine.

It was the early fifties and heroes were at the center of our lives. They were what we longed to be, believed we could be, the personas we assumed to negotiate the complicated process of growing up in the outwardly cheerful, optimistic environment of the Silent Generation. Heroes occupied our dreams.

When I was three or four, attentive to conversations, lying between my parents in their bed at night pretending to sleep, they would talk about the war.

In my mind, I traveled across the Atlantic Ocean for a conversation I had arranged by telephone with Adolf Hitler. A little girl traveling alone with her small dog, Trixie, would be able to persuade this villain to stop the war. I remember that in these waking dreams I'd be crossing the Atlantic on foot. I wasn't familiar with boats, and I thought of distance as the time it took to walk from our front porch to the mailbox or out back to Guy and Aida's house. Hitler lurked somewhere just beyond an ocean the size of our vegetable garden, in back of Guy and Aida's peeling white clapboard house, in a house very much like ours.

The Babies' Ward was as close as I came in my stay at Warm Springs to assembling an imaginary life within the real one.

Tommy Boy was in the first crib. I saw myself not as his mother, who lived in Atlanta and visited on weekends, but as his doctor. I was going to teach him to walk. His residual paralysis was similar to mine, his left side weakened by the disease, especially his leg; his right side was almost normal. On warm days I'd take Tommy Boy in my lap out of the Babies' Ward, out the side doors of Second Medical and across the quad where there was a basketball court, where kids played in wheelchairs most mornings before lunch if the weather was good. We'd sit on the edge of the court and I'd lift him onto the grass, leaning over my wheelchair so my grip around his upper body was secure, and then I'd teach him to take one step and then another.

"Walk, Tommy Boy," I'd say to him, and he'd give a huge, toothy smile and say the only word he could say besides "da," which was "walk." I had taught him that. My idea was that if he learned the word — if "walk" was imprinted on his brain — then he would be able in some mysterious way to correlate his muscles with the word and learn to walk in fact.

I told my mother this theory during one of our Sunday telephone calls, and she said she'd ask Dr. Nicholson whether a scientific correlation existed between language and action. But I could tell it didn't make a great deal of sense to her logical mind.

It did to Tommy Boy and me.

Before he left Warm Springs for the last time, in the early winter of my first year, he walked on his little fat legs from the crib where he'd been sleeping for almost a year into his mother's arms.

"Eleven steps," his mother said happily to his father. "Eleven big steps." And she swung him around in a circle.

I was in the Babies' Ward reading a story to Rosie when that happened.

"How did he learn to walk?" Tommy Boy's father asked Paisley Jean.

"I taught him," Paisley Jean said. "If there are traces of muscles, I can teach them to walk."

But Tommy Boy knew better and so did I, and that was what mattered. Only our time sitting next to the basketball court counted, my arms around his belly. Walk, I'd say, one foot in front of the other. And he did.

When I first saw Rosie, she was sitting in the corner of her crib chewing on a book, and Paisley Jean told me her name was Cynthia Ann and her mother was dead.

"Of polio," she said. "It hardly ever happens, but it happened to her mother, in Philadelphia, in an epidemic last March."

Usually I didn't find out personal information about the babies except from Paisley Jean, and then only if none of the other nurses was around. She liked to gossip about the private stories of children's lives. She particularly liked the tragedies and perhaps increased their troubles for my benefit if the ones they had didn't seem sufficient.

I was a willing listener, with a preference for dramatic stories, a tendency to exaggeration. But in the case of Rosie's mother, I believed Paisley Jean. The baby girl had the hollow look of a child with something missing, and I claimed her for my own.

"I will be your mommy," I'd whisper in her ear, my breath tickling her cheek so that she'd giggle.

I could not imagine my own life without a mother.

In second grade at Sidwell Friends, my classmate Elaine's mother had died of breast cancer over Christmas vacation, and Elaine had come back to school after New Year's with her black curly hair cut very short, close to the skull. Was that shearing her own doing in grief, I wondered, or had someone thought to cut her hair to call attention to her loss? I'd sit in reading class watching Elaine two seats away, slipping down in my own seat so I could stare without her knowing. To my amazement, she could read aloud without a quaver in her voice. Maybe she didn't love her mother the way I did mine. Or maybe she was covering up her sadness and one day might die of sadness in her sleep.

If my mother were not there to see me, I would not exist.

When I left the Babies' Ward every day at noon, in time to put Rosie back in her crib and get the lunch trays, I ached at having to let her go. She was always the last baby I held on my visits, the sweet dessert, my darling girl. I thought of myself as her mother.

I could recall afterward that Magnolia had her eyes on Violet Blue, that her jaw was clenched and her fingers were tight around the railing and her black eyes in the glance I got of them were flashing. She leaned her head down, grabbed Violet Blue's little fist, clamped her teeth on the fleshy fingers, and bit through the skin.

Paisley Jean shouted at me, the veins popping in her neck, her voice trembling, and the sound of baby voices in the room went silent except for the long wail coming from Violet Blue.

"Leave," Paisley Jean said. "Leave the ward now."

I didn't move. I saw blood coming from Violet Blue's finger, the look of surprise on Magnolia's face, felt Paisley Jean rush by me and pick up the bleeding baby.

"She make blood," Violet Blue said, holding her hand out for the nurse to see.

"You broke the skin," Paisley Jean said to Magnolia. "Do you *see* the blood?"

Magnolia looked up at her, shook her head, buried her face in her arm.

"She can't hear," I reminded Paisley Jean. "She doesn't know what you're saying."

"I've heard about her. Her mother's on the maid staff, right?" Paisley Jean asked, washing Violet Blue's bloody finger under the faucet in the corner of the room.

"Her name is Magnolia," I said.

"Magnolia." Paisley Jean put antiseptic on the bloody hand and wrapped it in gauze and tape. "What's her last name?"

"I don't know her last name," I said as Paisley Jean moved the rocking chair over next to Violet Blue's crib and rocked her. "Her mother works on my floor. I think she cleans."

"What are you doing being friends with a child like this anyway, Susan?" Paisley Jean asked.

I had lifted Magnolia back on my lap and she sat there quietly, her head hanging down as if she were expecting something more to happen.

I didn't know how to answer Paisley Jean. Magnolia was my friend. She needed to be my friend.

"Causing trouble is what you're doing," Paisley Jean answered for herself. "You ought to take this Magnolia back where you found her. You oughtn't be playing with her—you know that."

"I don't," I said, and I suppose my heart was beating hard because I did know. At least I was beginning to understand what was more alarming than the kind of trouble I was accustomed to getting into at school.

"Time you did know," Paisley Jean said. "She could have rabies, you know, and now she's bit Violet Blue."

"Dogs have rabies," I said.

"Dogs have rabies and they bite children and then the children die."

"She's not a dog," I said.

"No," Paisley Jean said quietly. "She's not a dog."

I didn't leave, and Paisley Jean didn't ask me to again. We sat there quietly while all around us those babies peered out of their cribs, waiting to see what would happen next, and Violet Blue nestled into Paisley Jean's arms.

After a while, Paisley Jean took off the bandage and checked to see if the bleeding had stopped, and then she wrapped Violet Blue's hand up again.

"What's going to happen?" I asked finally.

"Children have germs," she said. "The mouth is a dirty place, and I can't tell you what's going to happen until it happens."

"Maybe there's a medicine you can use on her hand," I said.

"Maybe," Paisley Jean said, looking at Magnolia, whose head was still hanging. "She's completely deaf?"

I nodded.

"What do you think would happen if I told Dr. Iler that a colored girl had bitten this precious one and broken the skin?"

"I don't know," I said.

"Yes, you do. You're from Washington, D.C., and you know what I'm talking about."

I couldn't bear it. I wrapped my arms around the skinny-boned girl, put her head in the crook of my neck.

"So what are you going to say to Dr. Iler?"

Paisley Jean sat for a long time, what felt like a long time anyway, before she answered. When she spoke, she wasn't looking at me. She was staring across the room at something, and when I followed her eyes, I saw they had rested on Tommy Boy sleeping in his crib.

"I'm going to ask Dr. Iler what to do with a child bite and show him Violet Blue's hand."

"And tell him it was Magnolia?" I asked. "You can tell him it was me. Tell him I just got mad at Violet's temper and bit her."

"I'm not going to tell him that, because it isn't true," she said, taking a deep breath. "I'm going to say one of the babies bit her because he was teething, and the fault was mine."

"But that's not true either," I said.

"I get to choose what I say, don't I?" Paisley Jean said. "And that's what I've chosen."

I left then. I didn't know what to say, didn't know whether I was relieved or felt worse than I would have if I'd taken the blame for what happened, since it was mine to take.

Upstairs, Magnolia's mother was at the other end of the hall with a pail and mop, cleaning the floor outside the Boys' Ward. Maybe she saw us come up, maybe she didn't. Maybe she didn't even know that Magnolia was gone from under the table. We'd been in the Babies' Ward for only a short time. I kissed Magnolia's cheek and she hopped off my lap and scrambled under the table, where she stayed, lying on her belly, burrowing her face in her arms.

When I came back after lunch, after my catechism lesson with Father James, Magnolia was gone, earlier than she usually left. Maybe she had asked to go home, or maybe her mother was finished work for the day. I didn't want to know.

Violet Blue was lying on the changing table when I went back to the Babies' Ward just before the dinner trays were delivered, and Paisley Jean was redressing her hand.

I had wanted to confess my sin to Father James that afternoon. But I didn't want to say "Forgive me, Father, for I have sinned" and for him to tell me to repeat a bunch of "Hail Mary full of grace"s so the sin would dissolve. I didn't really believe anything I said would make a difference.

I knew I had sinned. But I wasn't at all sure what, of the many things I might have done or did do that morning in the Babies' Ward with Magnolia, had been the sin.

I wheeled over to Paisley Jean.

"Thank you for what you did," I said.

"I did nothing but take care of my babies as I usually do."

"You didn't tell Dr. Iler it was my fault."

"Oh, that," she said. "I didn't think it was your fault."

But someplace in my thinking, I must have known that trouble didn't follow me around, pick me out of the crowd as a likely candidate, try my patience.

I pushed the limits.

The Body and the Blood

THE NIGHT BEFORE she left, my mother told me that chances were I'd have my first period at Warm Springs, although she hoped it wouldn't come until I was home again. But she had been early, maybe as young as ten, so I should expect it.

I didn't expect it, had no reason to think about it again, since it sounded such a strange phenomenon, difficult to imagine just by my mother's description. So when I started, in early November, I was stunned and fascinated and probably, by the account of others' experiences, also sad. But sadness was not a feeling I allowed myself until I was almost forty. In my mind, sadness had the weight of death, so I exterminated it whenever I felt its undertow slipping in under my skin.

However enigmatic by nature my mother was, she was direct about specifics, particularly about sex and the body, which had a different context in her mind than they seemed to have for the more fastidious mothers of my friends. Growing up, I thought her ease in talking about sex came from an open-minded Danish background untainted by American puritanism, but I now believe it simply had to do with her.

By the time I got my period, I had had long conversations with her about the pleasure of sex, and men and women, and the changes in the body of a girl. She had also left sanitary napkins and an elastic belt in my night table, next to the bedpan, so I got them out and put them on with curiosity and disgust.

Weird was how I felt that week. I didn't tell anyone, not even my mother at first. An unfamiliar combination of secrecy and exhibitionism overtook me almost immediately. I didn't know what to do with myself. In the long mirror on the door of the closet I shared with Caroline, I discovered I was getting fat. Rather, I was spreading. I'd gone to bed with my familiar bony body, all sharp edges and no flesh, and awakened in the process of expanding.

My body had been available for public scrutiny since I could remember. I was accustomed to lying on examining tables covered with nothing but a sheet, to the arrival of doctors, sometimes singly, sometimes in teams, who pulled the sheet off, poked and prodded, rarely even glancing at my face. I'd lie naked while they gathered around the table talking about me as if I were fair game. At the time, it didn't seem like a violation of privacy. I had never had a chance to develop a sense of modesty, so I wasn't aware of the loss of it.

Certain boundaries were perplexing and unclear. Since I was by nature a child who wanted to jump in the water whether or not I could swim, I needed help in this transition to *womanhood*, as it was delicately called when I was growing up, and the only person I would have been comfortable talking to wasn't there.

Three mornings a week I had catechism with Father James. I'd lie in bed at night, unable to sleep, and think of the Passion of Christ. In my dreams, He had the beautiful face of Father James and died on the cross for our sins, and I hoped to have many sins, to make His dying worthwhile.

After lights out, Caroline had difficulty getting comfortable, and I needed her to go to sleep so I could pray. I didn't want her to know that I was praying, something I had never done except for my regular plea to the galaxy for certainty: *Star light, star bright* . . .

I didn't want her to think I was that kind of girl, because she had told me that her parents thought Roman Catholics were disgusting.

"They have children one after the other like rabbits, is what my father told me," she said. "They don't even think about it."

On Sundays, Caroline was taken on her stretcher to the Methodist service, in the room where the movies were shown, and she hated it.

"Why do you go, then?" I asked.

"I go to be good," she replied in her definite way.

"You'd be good whether you went to church or not," I said, and she gave me one of her icy looks.

"You don't *know* that," she said.

What I did know was that my conversion to Catholicism had nothing to do with *good*.

I wanted to be transported.

At night when Caroline finally went to sleep, I prayed. She might have been awake, watching me through the slits of her eyes, but she never mentioned it, never said she saw me slip out of my bed into my wheelchair, my elbows propped on the bed, my hands together, my chin resting in the V made by my thumbs. I prayed to the Blessed Virgin. The vision on the inside of my eyelids was of myself in a white dress to the ankles, bare feet, my hair long and curly and black, and I am walking up the hill to Calvary, where Jesus is dying on the cross, and the sight of Him dying is wondrous. I stand under the cross next to the crouching, veiled Mary Magdalen and the Blessed Virgin, and the blood falling from His ankles stains my white dress.

I didn't tell Father James about my vision, only that I prayed, but I did ask him if there were any children on Calvary when Jesus died.

He said he doubted it. Children wouldn't have attended a crucifixion, wouldn't have been allowed to be there.

"But maybe an orphan," I said.

"Maybe an orphan," he said. "But I don't think so."

Every night I repeated the same prayer with a vision of Jesus on the cross, and just the vision of Jesus gave me a rush as if my own blood were accelerating.

Joey Buckley returned to the Boys' Ward from the sick patients' ward a week after I had watched him being taken away. I overheard Miss Riley talking about him to Dr. Iler, who said that Joey's situation had been "precarious," and so I asked Caroline the meaning of the word.

"I heard my friend Joey Buckley's condition was dangerous," I said later to Miss Riley.

"From whom did you hear that?"

"One of the nurses," I said.

"Well, he's fine now," Miss Riley said. "Perfectly fine and in the Boys' Ward, where you can't go."

I knew that, of course, but had no intention of obeying her prohibition.

"You could write him a letter, and I'll see that he gets it."

"Thank you," I said, turning my wheelchair around in the direction of my room.

It was almost three, I noted from the clock overhead. Miss Riley left at four.

When I got back, Caroline was gone, so she must have been taken to x-ray or physical therapy, since she hardly ever left the room except for a special occasion, like the Saturday movies.

I got the Alabama cap out of the top drawer of my dresser and put it on low on my forehead, sticking my bangs under the band. In the mirror on our closet door I noted that in spite of my body's expanding, I still looked like myself in a baseball cap. I sucked in my cheeks, assuming the pouty, lippy look I'd seen in the movies.

And then I must have had a sudden inspiration and took hold of it, ignoring the inevitable consequences until later.

In the drawer of my bedside table, among other assorted things, I'd stuffed the elastic belt that secured a sanitary napkin. I took the pink elastic with hooks at the front and back and slipped it over my head, where it hung like a necklace to my breastbone on the outside of my shirt. In the mirror, which I checked again before I left for the Boys' Ward, I was pleased with my reflection, with the addition of this elastic jewelry around my neck, the baseball cap framing my face. I headed out the door in the direction of the Boys' Ward, feeling almost pretty.

Miss Riley, who should have gone off duty, was talking to Dr. Iler as I wheeled by, and I thought she might have caught sight of me out of the corner of her eye. I pushed the down button on the elevator so she'd think I was going downstairs, and when the elevator doors opened, I went down the hall in the direction of the Boys' Ward.

In spite of everything Father James had told me about the Virgin Mary, I couldn't get excited about her. She seemed to me a sweet, gentle, pleasant mother who had lost her son, although He wasn't exactly dead — not *dead is dead,* as I had thought about death before the process of my conversion. But on the whole she was kindly, dutiful, sort of beautiful in her pictures, but of no particular interest to me.

Jesus was the one who captured my imagination. Not the red-haired version of Jesus either, who seemed pale and sickly, but the darker one I imagined hanging by nails hammered through his skin and bone, not making a fuss about the pain.

Nevertheless, I had taken seriously the importance of the Virgin to Father James and wanted to please him. So I told him that my name was Mary, that I was called by my middle name, Mary, because of my admiration for the Blessed Virgin or the Blessed Mother.

I doubt now that Father James believed me, but either he liked me, and I think he did, or I was of interest to him, in part because he was of interest to himself and I was an excellent listener.

At eleven, I looked older than I was, angular features with high cheekbones, full lips, dark eyes, which in pictures from that time give off a sense of age. In photographs, even when I was a baby, my brow is always furrowed. As a result of that, or of my great interest in him, Father James got in the habit of telling me personal things, which I doubt he told anybody else.

I knew he had been married before he became a priest, that he had grown up in northern Ireland — "Belfast," he told me — and left because of the failure of his marriage, which led him to the priesthood. Eventually he changed the story, or else I had misunderstood it in the first place. He later said he had become a priest when his young wife had died.

For almost a year I didn't know which story was true, although I was surprised by the discrepancy and preferred to think his wife had died. Somehow her dying reflected better on Father.

What interested me was that he had been married at all and that he had told two stories about the end of it. It made him someone more than a priest, and the mystery of who that was obsessed me.

As I've said, I thought a lot about death — more, according to Father James, than usual for an eleven-year-old who had had polio. I didn't talk about it, certainly not to my parents, especially my mother, who would have been distressed to know that my sunny exterior could not be counted on as fact.

Or perhaps my mother did know and that was part of the secret dance we did together.

One morning during a lull in our catechism class, when Father James, distracted, was looking out the window, I told him that I thought death was his business.

The thought had come to me on a day when we had been discussing the Holy Ghost. I understood the Holy Ghost to be the Spirit of God, and as such He could not materialize in the flesh. But a ghost was an apparition that had once been alive and now was dead, and God as a ghost didn't make sense. Or, rather, if it did, my fear about existence would be confirmed.

Invisibility was what troubled me. It was possible that I could be conscious of my own presence and not be seen by others, and that would indicate that I didn't exist.

Or was my own consciousness sufficient proof of life?

That was the kind of thinking that came about with too much solitude.

"I was wondering whether we would have God if we never died," I said, bringing Father James's attention back to the room.

"But we do die," Father James said.

"That's what I mean."

"I don't understand what you're asking me," he said, leaning over the desk, brushing the hair out of my eyes.

"I'm asking you to explain God to me," I said.

"That's what we're doing together in catechism classes, but God is not an explanation."

"But I *want* to believe in Him."

Since my childhood need for promises of safety from my father, I had been an uneasy sleeper. Some nights at Warm Springs I didn't sleep at all, lying on my back, my eyes on the ceiling, or on my side looking out the window beside the bed, or with the pillow covering my face to cancel out the light.

And tumbling over and over in my mind, keeping me wide awake even as I tried with growing desperation to fall asleep, was the prayer that Grandma Richards used to insist I repeat after her when I was very young: *Now I lay me down to sleep, I pray the Lord my soul to keep.* I repeated only that much of the prayer, refusing to continue: *If I should die before I wake, I pray the Lord my soul to take.*

I didn't want to die or to think there was a chance of it. I didn't want my soul taken. It wasn't God's to have.

"Sometimes you're better at imagining than thinking," Father James said when I told him that story. "But as to death, I think of myself in the business of living, not dying."

I cannot for the life of me understand now how I had the nerve or stupidity or exhibitionism to wear a sanitary belt around my neck, in full view of nurses and doctors and eighteen adolescents in the Boys' Ward. It occurs to me now, considerably more embarrassed for myself in reflection than I was then, that the gesture was an announcement of desire.

I went into the Boys' Ward as if they expected me. In the far corner of the room, Miss Barnes was fixing the IV of one of the boys, and Joey was propped up on pillows in the first bed, and a boy I'd never met was leaning on his crutches, looking out the window.

I pushed my wheelchair across the room to Miss Barnes, so I could announce myself before she had a chance to ask me to leave.

"I need to see my friend Joey Buckley," I said.

"Ask Miss Riley." She was concentrating on slipping the needle into the boy's vein. "She's in charge."

"You're going to get in trouble," the boy in the bed next to Joey's said. "Girls aren't allowed."

"I'm allowed," I said.

"Who says?" the boy asked.

I pulled my wheelchair up beside Joey's bed.

"Miss Barnes," I said.

"The baseball cap looks good on you," Joey said. He was pale and thin and fragile against the white pillow.

"I wear it every day," I said. "It's my favorite."

"I guess you know I've been sick," he said.

"I was here when they took you away."

"I had blood poisoning from the incision they did when I had my stabilization, and they don't know why because it's never happened before, but it happened to me, and so I was really sick."

"And you're okay now?"

"I won't be allowed up in my wheelchair for a while," he said. "But I'm not sick any longer, and the year after next I'll be playing football, I think."

I wheeled my chair between Joey's bed and the one beside it.

"Hey, girl." The boy in the next bed swung his legs over the side. "What's that thing around your neck?" He called to another boy to look. "Ask the girl what's that thing she's wearing, Joey."

"It's a necklace," I replied.

"An elastic necklace?" the boy next to Joey asked.

Joey was looking at me and I didn't know exactly what to say, already sorry I had the sanitary belt around my neck, but not sure what to do with it or what I could possibly say about it.

"I've seen that kind of thing before in my house," the boy next to Joey said, "and it's *not* a necklace."

"Shut up," Joey said.

"Don't tell me to shut up."

"Then leave her alone."

The boys were yelling at each other. Miss Barnes had finished inserting the IV needle and was headed in my direction.

"No shouting," she said, coming up behind my wheelchair. "What's going on?"

"We're fighting about this girl and the necklace she's got hanging on her," the boy said.

Before I had a chance to speak, to turn my chair around and explain myself or leave, the nurse had caught hold of the sanitary belt and pulled it off.

"What is your name?" she asked, dropping the belt in her pocket.

"Susan," the boy said. "Isn't that her name, Joey?"

"You'll be coming with me, Susan."

Father James took me to the office where we had catechism class and shut the door. The office belonged to Dr. Iler, and photographs of children lined the walls, but I hadn't noticed the pictures before this afternoon, when I couldn't look at Father James and had to concentrate my attention on the walls.

The children, four of them, all girls, were blond with wavy hair in pageboys. They sat on a cement garden bench in one of the pictures, their hands folded in their laps, their eyes on the camera. In another picture they leaned against a tree holding hands. In another they were climbing the same tree, one on a low branch, two standing on a higher branch, the fourth at the bottom of the tree.

Next to the girls was a picture of President Franklin Roosevelt sitting on the edge of a dock, his legs hanging like the legs of all the children I had seen at Warm Springs: thin, lifeless, the feet dropping, curling in a half-moon, pointing toward each other.

"Are those President Roosevelt's children?" I asked as a way of putting off the talk I was there to have with Father James.

He was writing in a notebook on the desk, and it occurred to me that he was no more interested in talking to me about what had happened in the Boys' Ward than I was interested in talking to him.

"Those are Dr. Iler's children," he said.

"I guess from the picture that President Roosevelt had the same kind of polio as Joey Buckley, didn't he?"

Father James looked over at the photograph.

"He couldn't walk, if that's what you mean by the same."

"Joey is expecting to walk," I said, falling silent.

There were many photographs of Roosevelt in the halls of the Warm Springs Foundation, and most of them were formal and taken above the waist. There were a few of him standing with someone supporting him, like a human crutch. There was one showing him in a wheelchair, and the one in Dr. Iler's office, Roosevelt without his leg braces, his long legs exposed, swinging free as skinned chickens hanging in a butcher shop.

I know now what I didn't at the time, the lengths he went to in order to conceal that he was crippled — that he was carried through the back doors of the buildings where he was giving speeches, arriving early at events so he could be seated before the crowd arrived; that he was hoisted down shafts and fire escapes, lifted into and out of boats and trains and planes. I understand the trust he needed to have in those who protected him, the pain he endured to stand or walk while holding on to the arms of others so he would not be perceived as disabled, the courage to pretend that he was fine — his head thrown back, his cigarette holder clamped in the side of his mouth, his great, long laugh, intrinsic to his character as a leader at once solitary and public.

In the spring of 1997, the Franklin D. Roosevelt Memorial, forty years in the making, was dedicated amid considerable controversy by President Bill Clinton.

There was no wheelchair in the initial memorial.

After lobbying by the National Organization on Disability, President Clinton announced that he would send legislation to Congress to modify the memorial, to present Roosevelt not as the public knew him but as his intimates did, certainly those who had known him at Warm Springs. The new memorial, which includes a wheelchair, was dedicated in January 2001, and it recognizes that who Roosevelt was and what he achieved could not be separated from his damaged body.

I don't know which memorial I prefer, the one depicting Roosevelt's "splendid deception" as a strong, healthy figure of a leader, or the one with the addition of his wheelchair. By all accounts he would have preferred the first memorial to the second. Our perceptions about disability have changed since then, and that in part is because of Roosevelt. It's also true that he was a privileged man who served as president in a time of depression and war, and was seen as a man of the people, a perception made possible in part because it was visibly clear that privilege had not freed him from the trials of ordinary men.

It was November of 1950, and I had been in Warm Springs for three months, and it was only three weeks since my mother had left.

I was beginning to assemble a life alone. In my imagination

it grew beyond its reality but included Father James and Joey Buckley and Caroline and Magnolia and the babies and President Roosevelt.

At home in Washington, my family would be gathering for dinner, my mother in the kitchen with Jeffie, who would tell her about his day and the boys who beat him up on the playground and the girls he loved. Grandma Richards would be making cookies, and General Beauregard would be sleeping on the sofa, since there was no one in the living room to remove him. My father would be home late or not at all because he was traveling. There were not enough people in our house, I thought. Even if I were at home, our family was too small.

In my passport case, under my T-shirt, there was an unopened letter from my mother, which had come on the day of my humiliation. She wrote me every day, my father wrote once a week, and Harold Ickes sent a letter from time to time with news of the miseries of sixth grade. Occasionally my little brother wrote, scrawling across the page at my mother's instruction: *Dear Suzie, I am fine. Beau is fine. Mom and Dad is fine. Grandma is fine. Love, Jeffie. P.S. Granfer Swindells died yesterday in his own house while I was playing with my friends in the Swindellses' back yard.*

My mother's letters were chatty until the end, which was always the same: *P.S. Remember, I know you will, you can do anything you want to do with your life, be anyone you want to be. M.*

Father James closed the notebook and leaned back in his chair, looking at me.

"*Infra dignitatem.*" He folded his hands on the desk. "You don't know Latin."

I shook my head.

"Dignity?"

"I know the word dignity," I said.

He leaned across the desk.

"One of the things I've noticed in the years I've worked with polios is shame. Do you know what I mean by shame?" He answered the question himself. "Something like disgrace or humiliation. Polios feel ashamed because they had polio. As if they are to blame for it."

I wasn't sure I understood what he was saying, only that it seemed to be specific to me.

"Do you feel ashamed?" he asked.

The moment was weighted with a kind of importance.

"Because I had polio?"

He nodded.

"I've made my family unhappy. If that's what you mean by ashamed. I feel destructive."

"Destructive."

He said it as a matter of fact, as if he were collecting a list of applicable vocabulary.

I was uncertain how this conversation was unfolding. Was the subject my visit to the Boys' Ward in the pink elastic necklace, or was Father James trying to avoid a delicate issue because he was a priest?

"What have you destroyed?"

He had a habit of sitting very straight and still, his palms pressed flat together, his chin resting on the tops of his fingers, his water-blue eyes bright under weary eyelids.

"A lot of things," I said. "I'll bring you a list of things I've destroyed if you'd like to see it."

"Miss Riley thinks you need to be in school because you're bored."

"I don't want to be in school except a regular one," I said. "School would mean me and a tutor sitting in a room together, and I don't want that. Besides, I have catechism with you, where I learn about everything except spelling, and I already know how to spell."

"Then," he began, pushing a book across the desk for my second catechism lesson of the day, "we'll start this afternoon with the Holy Ghost."

*　　*　　*

That night, a cold and silver night, not enough covers over me to stay warm, I thought about the Holy Ghost. If I lay very still with my eyes closed, with my mind on little things like Clark bars and Grapette soda and the list in my Survival Notebook, the Holy Ghost might slip through the window glass and I wouldn't recognize Him except as warm air moving over my body, slipping through the layers of skin into my blood.

Thanksgiving Afternoon

MOST DAYS AFTER my mother went home to Washington, I got not one but two envelopes from her, one with a cozy, chatty letter and the second with newspaper clippings from the Washington newspapers, sometimes photographs from fashion magazines or recipes. My mother was not an every-day cook — we went to restaurants more than most families in our neighborhood — but when she did cook, when she did anything, she did it to perfection. She loved recipes. She would sit in bed leaning against an avalanche of pillows reading cookbooks — *Fannie Farmer* was her particular favorite — and historical novels and mysteries.

Sometimes now, I imagine her childhood from the photographs I have. In a tent in northern Wisconsin, sleeping on a cot with her parents. In St. Louis when she was nine, her mother very ill, her father traveling. "Take care of your mother while I'm gone," he'd said. "She isn't feeling well." Her mother died under her care. In Urbana where her grandparents lived, she shared a suite in a rooming house with her father, a widower in his mid-thirties. In the house of her stepmother after her father had died in an accident at the Urbana Mill, the wheat-processing mill that he owned.

Of course she would love recipes, as substitutes for the meals she had missed growing up.

Early in November, she began to send me menus for Thanksgiving that she had clipped from the newspaper, and the idea was for me to decide which dishes she would make. We always had the same thing for Thanksgiving: turkey and stuffing made with butter and bread crumbs and onions, green beans and Brussels sprouts, mashed potatoes with gravy, and apple pie with cheese and mince pie with hard sauce and pumpkin pie with whipped cream. I was not a big eater, but I liked stuffing with gravy and pumpkin pie, and I loved reading recipes in the same calming way I loved reading the words in the hymnal and leafing through the photographs of paintings in art books.

After the recipes started to come with the newspaper stories, I'd sit up in bed while Caroline was reading and go through my mother's suggestions. It became one of our brief but predictable dances. I knew we would have the same Thanksgiving we always had, and I wanted it that way, but I'd write back choosing creamed onions or chocolate mousse or oysters Rockefeller, and she'd write to say the creamed onions and the mousse, et cetera, et cetera, sounded delicious.

I read the newspaper stories after the recipes.

On one occasion, my mother sent me a story about Pope Pius XII's announcement of a new Catholic Church dogma that included the bodily Assumption of the Blessed Virgin Mary, with a note in her scrawly handwriting: "I don't know how the Blessed Virgin could allow this to happen."

In conversation, my mother always treated me as an equal conspirator. Sometimes I understood what she was saying, sometimes not, but I'd always pretend to know.

When I asked Father James about the bodily Assumption, hoping to impress him with my knowledge of dogma, he explained that the Blessed Virgin was now like Jesus — resurrected and in heaven is what I remember him saying — and the new doctrine was important for me to understand.

Heaven held no interest for me. It was too perfect a place. Just the thought of being there with Jesus, and now the Blessed Virgin, as well as quite a few other good people — it all struck me as a high-security prison. But I was fascinated with the idea of bodily

Assumption, of floating up into the sky, through the clouds like a balloon, fully dressed and perfectly intact.

I had never shown an interest in politics, and was always more taken with feature stories that had to do with the trials of one person's life rather than the general condition of mankind. But that fall I received many clips about the state of affairs in Washington and one new book, which I didn't read until years later, called *The Lottery*, by Shirley Jackson.

"Read the story 'The Lottery,' " my mother wrote. "It's frightening."

Caroline, more bookish than I, read "The Lottery" instead and told me it was about a town that decides every year to stone one person, selected by a drawing of names. Caroline agreed with my mother that the story was scary, and added that nothing like that could ever happen in the town in Illinois where she lived.

Only in New England.

I learned a lot from Caroline that first year.

My parents, particularly my father, were horrified by the witch-hunting career of Senator Joseph McCarthy. Just before I left for Warm Springs, Congress passed the anti-Communist McCarran Internal Security Act, setting drastic curbs on the rights of those accused of being "subversive." I knew from my mother that my father would have joined the Communist Party when he was at Ohio State, except that he was the editor of the college newspaper and not a joiner in any case, and just the way she spoke, either her excitement or perhaps her anger at what was going on, made me worry for my father's safety.

I knew that early in the winter of 1950, McCarthy had falsely charged that there were a couple of hundred card-carrying Communists in the State Department. Before I left for Warm Springs, we had frequent dinner conversations about Senator McCarthy, usually including a couple of visiting drunks my father had taken in, and the talk would go on and on past my bedtime, past my tolerance for adult conversation.

"Do you mean these Communists could be killed?" I'd asked my father at the table one night.

"Their careers will be over," my father had said. "Their lives will be ruined."

One of the newspaper stories I received from my mother in early November that year had to do with a Puerto Rican nationalist's attempt to assassinate President Truman at Blair House, where Truman was staying.

"Such a lot is happening in Washington," she wrote, "but nothing on our street except news from the Bowmans about Korea."

Our next-door neighbor had gone off to fight in the Korean War, and my mother sent an article from the local paper saying that he was back and at Walter Reed Hospital, recovering from his wounds.

And once on a June day before I arrived at Warm Springs, while walking with my mother in Georgetown, we passed a row house near 34th Street with a policeman leaning against the wall.

"That house belongs to Alger Hiss," my mother said, peering in to see if anyone was at home. "He's in trouble for being a Russian spy."

"Spy" was part of my vocabulary. It was in common use in the early fifties.

As I sat in a hospital bed with a light focused on my reading, especially the mail from my mother, Washington seemed a very long way from a village in Georgia. Caroline was across from me, lost in her Nancy Drew or Charles Dickens, the lights in the corridors had been dimmed, and the night sounds of clicking footsteps on linoleum as the nurses gave out meds and bedpans and juice were background music. In the stories from home, Washington had become a dangerous city, and I lost sight of my memory of streets lined with shade trees, of rolling green lawns and children and bicycles and dogs, even the occasional horse trotting up and down the streets where I had been growing up — a small, provincial, segregated southern town where the central offices of the United States government happened to be located.

The hospital had notified my mother about the episode with the sanitary belt, and she had talked to me about it during one of our Sunday afternoon phone calls. It was important to me that my father not find out, and she told me that on this occasion she wouldn't tell him.

I was never nervous with my mother, never felt as if there were anything I could do to upset her, nothing specific that would cause her to raise her voice or take on a tone of disapproval.

And so it was with the story of the sanitary belt.

Miss Riley had been the one to call her.

"I wasn't surprised," my mother said to me in her quiet, confident voice. "What does a girl do at eleven years old without help from an adult?" She said it wasn't my fault. "I told Miss Riley that *she* might have been of some help to you with your first period."

It made me smile.

But I didn't try to go to the Boys' Ward for the rest of the month and didn't see Joey Buckley at all.

I had planned to leave on the Sunday before Thanksgiving, on a train to Atlanta where I would meet my father, who was flying there to pick me up. I made a list of the clothes I was going to take. I expected my cast to be removed, although I knew I would be able to walk on only one leg and with crutches. But the hospital was going to send me home with a folding wheelchair.

I had written Harold Ickes that I'd be coming home, and he wrote back to say he hated sixth grade, in case I was interested, and would I be able to go horseback riding on his farm when I got there?

The plan was, I'd be home for a week and then my mother would bring me back to Warm Springs by train and I'd stay until Christmas. Maybe, I allowed myself to think, she would stay with me.

My cast was due to come off the Friday before I left to go home. When the nurse came to take me to the plaster room, I was in the supply closet playing a game of old maid with Magnolia.

I had been in a cast for three months, and that seemed a very long time, long enough for my leg to restore itself to a leg entirely changed from the one I remembered.

I daydreamed of riding a horse with my new leg, of galloping across the fields of the Ickes farm. Galloping was something I'd never done but could imagine.

I knew how to ride. When I was nine, my mother sent me for two months to the same sleep-away camp in Wells River, Vermont, where she had gone as a young girl. It was an old-fashioned camp with swimming and riding and tennis and canoeing — no motorboats or water skis, but arts and crafts, music, and a daily life of disciplined togetherness. I loved it there.

My mother was from a camping family. Her Danish father had owned two camps in northern Wisconsin. To reach the camps, it was necessary to portage canoes, and my mother lived there for the long summer, June to September, from the time she was born until her mother died, when her father sold the camps and moved back to Urbana.

When I look back, with the perspective of the mother I've been, and think about the courage it must have taken for my mother to let me go at nine, with her history of loss — her mother, her father, and almost, on a couple of occasions, her only daughter — I'm amazed that she sent me away from her watchful eye.

But she had made up her mind that I be treated as an ordinary girl, with no fewer expectations.

I went away outfitted for every sport, my name sewn in my uniforms. I had extra sweaters to stay warm at night, since I was so skinny; child's rubbers over my orthopedic shoes so I could stand on the tennis court and learn to return balls; jodhpurs my mother had made to fit over my brace for riding. My father, who had lived in a cottage next to a trotters' barn in New Philadelphia, Ohio, knew about horses and thought it was risky for me to ride. I could be thrown and then what? I probably would be thrown. A horse would know I was an easy toss.

My mother disagreed.

"She'll be *sitting* on the horse," she insisted. "She doesn't need to walk to ride a horse."

In fact, although my mother was not a rider and didn't realize that legs actually counted in horseback riding, it turned out she was right. I was a good rider and discovered enough muscle in my upper thighs to hold on. And the horses weren't fond of my brace, so I learned to use that to advantage. I did fall off, since I was something of a one-sided rider, but I was young and learned to fall.

You entered the plaster room and were hit with the smell of wet plaster and rancid flesh and a cloud of plaster dust. Casts were always being taken off and replaced, but this visit was my first and I was thrilled. There was an air of excitement in the room; this was the first step toward going home.

I sat up on the stretcher and the medical technician turned on the handsaw and sliced the cast open on either side.

"I cut this off," the technician explained, "and the doctor comes and we take a look and another x-ray and then the doc will tell you what next."

He cut the gauze inside the plaster, lifted off the top of the cast, dropped it in the trash, and left me sitting on the stretcher while he moved on to the next cast, on a boy I'd seen in the Boys' Ward in a body cast.

I don't know exactly what I expected to see when my bad leg was lifted out of the cast and I saw my reconstructed foot for the first time. Probably a matching leg.

When I tried to lift my leg out of the half-shell of cast, it didn't move. That was the first sign.

I leaned over to examine my foot, which was double the size of the foot that had gone into the cast in the first place, and I could tell that any trace of flesh on my right leg had disappeared.

Dr. Iler arrived late and in a hurry. He looked at me, took my chin in his hand, turned my face one way and then the other.

"You must be eating your grits," he said.

"You mean I'm fat?"

"You look healthy," he said. "You were too skinny when you got here."

He lifted my leg out of the cast.

"I'm going home for Thanksgiving," I said, taking the offensive, as I was in the habit of doing, stating what I hoped would happen as fact.

My ankle was bloody and swollen. My foot, puffed up as it was, looked like a more extreme deformity than I had before.

"I'm sending you to x-ray," Dr. Iler said, "and then we'll talk."

In hospitals, you wait and wait. I was accustomed to that. At Warm Springs, because the days went on so long, waiting for x-rays or cast removal or a doctor's appointment actually had a sense of adventure. At least something was going to happen. Some change from the sameness of the days.

Late in the afternoon, still on the stretcher, my newborn leg lying in a half-cast, I was taken to another room, next to x-ray. The picture of my new leg was on the wall, lit from behind.

"There it is," Dr. Iler said, coming in the door. "You're in good shape, a great success. One of the best." He pointed to the stabilized ankle on the back-lit picture, the pin, the re-formed foot. "Perfect."

"But pretty swollen, isn't it?"

"That's to be expected," he said, lifting the foot very gently in his hand, and the way he touched me was a hint. I understood that everything was not exactly as he had hoped.

"So I'll be ready to start physical therapy when I get back from Thanksgiving?"

"Not yet," he said. "You're not quite cooked. We're putting you back in a cast."

He patted my leg.

"So what happens now?" I asked, although I already knew that nothing was about to happen — no change, a new cast, more weeks to go, the same day-after-day inventing my own excitement.

I allowed the disappointment to slip quickly through my mind, in and out, so I was ready for what Dr. Iler said next, defended against it, already planning the rest of the month.

"I guess the plan has changed," I said.

"You won't be going home for Thanksgiving, if that's what you mean by changed," he said.

On the telephone with my mother, I was full of high cheer.

"Everyone tells me Thanksgiving at Warm Springs is so great, that I'll love it," I said.

I don't remember whether she offered to come down or not, because my decision was made, and if she had offered, I would have told her: "Don't come. I'm happy to be here for Thanksgiving, I mean it, and lots of other kids are here without their parents, and probably I'll be home for Christmas."

That's what I would have said, primed for optimism. I'm sure I never let my voice break. Never even thought it might.

I wonder now whether my high spirits hurt her feelings, whether she wanted to be needed as I certainly needed her, whether we were simply locked in that old two-step in which we didn't tell the real truth because we were afraid to hurt each other.

In writing this book, I have thought that I might have cheated her out of being a part of this lonely life I had without her by seeming as if I were enjoying it, reveling in the absence of her company. That if I'd shown a flicker of hesitation, she would have come to Warm Springs to spend Thanksgiving with me, grateful to be wanted.

But I didn't retread these years when she was alive, and perhaps she would not have remembered how she felt, so I can only imagine, as happens with memory and what we make of it.

After my conversation with my parents about Thanksgiving, I made a plan. I would put down roots. This was my home now, and the kind of spinning around the hospital that I'd been doing to fill the days — moving through the Babies' Ward, sneaking into the Boys' Ward, doing catechism with Father James — was not sufficient to a permanent life.

I didn't have the problems of the other children in Second Medical. Most of them, almost all of them, needed every bit of reserve to get better. I had free time. Many had come to Warm Springs in desperation, with small goals, and I had come with the expectation of returning to *real* life as an ordinary girl.

I was ashamed among these brave and damaged children. I needed to earn my keep.

It surprises me now, in these very different times, to think that we believed our lives to be morally balanced, that the good was rewarded and the failures punished. I was a true believer in this. In part it was my age, in part the age in which we were living, the forties and fifties.

Reading recently about Roosevelt, I was struck to discover that he regarded infantile paralysis and the possible end of his political career as punishment for his infidelity with Lucy Mercer. So that kind of feeling about morality and consequences was not uncommon even among sophisticated, intelligent people.

A confidence in checks and balances is an easy way to live, and I set out, that day after my cast was removed, to even the score. If I was lucky, as I certainly had been, then I had a duty to compensate for unearned good fortune. Or worse trouble lay ahead.

I made arrangements with Miss Riley to distribute and empty bedpans everywhere but the Boys' Ward. That was my morning job. I'd take the hot bedpans out of the sterilizer and go from room to room, to all the private rooms where children with more severe cases of polio were in residence, and then to the Girls' Ward and to some of the rooms at the other end of the corridor, beyond the Boys' Ward, where adults were in private or semiprivate rooms. Then I'd pick up the bedpans, a slow process, one at a time, the bedpan balanced in my lap, driving the wheelchair carefully so the sloshing urine stayed mostly in the pan. I'd dump the contents and put the soiled pan back in the sterilizer.

I can't say why — and that I was permitted by Miss Riley to do this job and wanted to do it is curious to me now — but it was entirely satisfactory work.

Every afternoon, I delivered the mail, so my life was carefully ordered: bedpans and then babies, followed by catechism and lunch and mail.

"I don't have any time for school," I told Father James when he recommended a tutor so I'd have a goal during my stay. "Miss Riley knows that I'm busy."

"What do your parents say?" he asked, concerned because most of the children in Second Medical who were not actually sick were being tutored.

"I haven't talked to them about it," I said.

I had no intention of bringing it up.

I'd seen the tutor. She worked with Caroline three times a week in math and reading, and even Caroline, who never criticized people, had nothing good to say about her.

But one afternoon between the end of my Thanksgiving plans and the actual celebration of Thanksgiving, Miss Forkman, the tutor, arrived in my room with a pile of books to say that arrangements had been made for me to be tutored three times a week.

"By whom?" I asked.

"I was called," Miss Forkman said, taking a seat beside my bed, where I was eating lunch. "So I suppose your parents made the arrangements."

I sensed we were off to a bad start already.

"When I finish lunch, I do the mail," I said.

"I spoke to Miss Riley and she said you could do the mail later."

She had brought a sixth-grade social studies textbook, an English grammar book, and a mathematics text.

"These are the books we'll be working on," she said and, handing me the social studies text, asked me to read to her so she could check my reading ability.

Miss Forkman was probably forty and maybe even attractive, although I remember her as very old, with a tank build, a wiry bun on top of her head, red lipstick, and short legs.

After the first class, I called my mother. I never called my mother during the week. It was difficult to make long distance calls, because I had to go to the first-floor offices and get help placing the calls, and the secretary didn't like to do it during the week. But this, I told her, was an emergency.

My mother said she hadn't been the one to make the arrangements. In fact, she didn't particularly care whether or not I had tutoring. She cared only that I get better and come home, which was just what I wanted to hear.

My mother had mixed feelings about school. Even when I finally returned to Washington and entered seventh grade at Alice Deal Junior High, where I received too many failing grades, I never felt pressure from her to do well. She had been homeschooled by her father, an academic before he bought the Urbana Mill, who distrusted the school system and objected to its insistence that she write with her right hand. My father, on the other hand, believed that school was a job and I should do it well, and when I didn't, his response was silence.

I chose to go with my mother and dismissed Miss Forkman after the first day.

On my mail route, I made friends. I'd arrive in a room with a lapful of mail and, especially in the Girls' Ward, I'd go from bed to bed and listen. I wasn't the only patient in a wheelchair. There were a number of us who were able to go to the candy store or wander around the foundation grounds or visit rooms. But I had a need to fill my day so there were no empty hours, a fear of loneliness — a kind of desperation is what I think in retrospect. If a white space loomed in the distance of a day, I'd have no barricade against homesickness.

"I understand you got rid of the tutor," Father James said.

"My mother didn't make arrangements for me to have tutoring," I replied. "So I don't know how the tutor got there in the first place."

"I sent her," Father James said.

I should not have been surprised but I was, and humiliated and hurt. Father James was my confidant, my spiritual instructor, my friend. And in my daydreams, he was also what I could conceive of as a lover — his hand on my wrist, on my hair, on the top of my head, his blue, blue eyes focused on me, sufficient to my capacity at eleven to imagine love.

I flew out of his office as fast as an antique wooden and wicker wheelchair could move, down the corridor, down the elevator, out the front door, across the courtyard, past Georgia Hall, and down the hill to the candy store, where I bought a Clark bar, a Grapette soda, and cheese puffs and ate them, one after the other, while parked in a corner next to the building, tears pouring down my cheeks.

Father James found me with Rosie. I had gone to the Babies' Ward for solace, which is what I found there — those needy babies, their arms outstretched, their eyes darting after me wherever I went. Paisley Jean allowed me to bundle Rosie into a soft yellow snowsuit and cap and, since it was a sunny day, take her out to the courtyard. She sat on my lap, her head against my shoulder, her soft cheek next to mine, and I rode her up and down the paths. She was able to sit, but she couldn't move her rag-doll legs, so Paisley Jean had tied a towel around her waist and mine to keep her from falling off my lap while I wheeled her.

Father James kneeled beside my wheelchair, his hand on the wheel so I wouldn't try to get away.

"I can't talk now," I said quietly.

"I am sorry," he said, his delicate hand gripping the arm of my chair. "I misunderstood."

What was it that he misunderstood? About the arrangement for a tutor and my embarrassment that he thought of me as such a child? About my love for him? About the girl I was, different from the one I seemed to be?

I turned my head away so he wouldn't see that I'd been crying and take pleasure in the possibility that it might have had to do with him.

On Thanksgiving Day it rained.

In Washington, my parents and Jeffie and Grandma Richards were having dinner at our house. They had invited the Bowmans from next door, whose son had been in Korea. My aunt Janet and uncle Joe and their children would come, and there would probably be a couple of inebriated journalists and some lost soul my father had happened to meet who didn't have a place to go for dinner. Such occasions at our house were probably replicated in nuclear families all over the transient city, people pulling together a facsimile of the Thanksgiving they remembered from their hometowns, where everyone was family.

Caroline's parents asked me to have Thanksgiving dinner with them at the cottage where Mrs. Slover stayed on the foundation grounds, but my plan was to go to Thanksgiving with the rest of the hospital in the hope of finding Joey Buckley among the children who had not gone home for the holiday.

In my mind, Joey had a full life. He wasn't exactly a romantic figure — although I reserved that possibility — but he was a constant companion, and I transmitted my thoughts and fears and worries to him in a kind of one-sided telepathic communication.

After picking up the bedpans — which had to be done on Thanksgiving the same as any other day, though there were fewer patients — I spent the morning in the Children's Ward.

Rosie was ill. The doctor on call, who came from town — probably a general practitioner, not an orthopedic doctor — was examining her when I went into the ward. Paisley Jean made me wait outside until he finished.

"She's sickly," Paisley Jean said after the doctor left and I started my rounds of the ward. "She's been this way since she came here, and her father tells us that it's because her mother's dead, but I think it's because she's sickly."

She had a virus, Paisley Jean said, and they were moving her to isolation so the other babies wouldn't catch it, and as the orderly pushed her crib through the ward and passed me, Rosie reached her arms in the air in my direction.

"Can I follow?" I asked.

"Absolutely not," Paisley Jean said. "You have to tend to some rules."

After I finished with Sue Sue, I wheeled over to her desk.

"Where are you going for Thanksgiving dinner?" I asked.

"Here," Paisley Jean said. "I'm on duty."

"Maybe I can stay and help you."

"I don't think so," she said.

Paisley Jean went on filling in the charts, her head down, her fingers running through her hair, her pen in and out of her mouth. I think now that she may have liked my company, that she enjoyed satisfying my curiosity with information, and that the other nurses were dutiful and dull. Dull was her word for them, and I took it as a compliment that I was not.

What I wanted to know from her was everything about Rosie.

"She's ten months old and her mama died in June and she's got older siblings and her dad takes care of them someplace in Pennsylvania."

"How do you know she's sickly?" I asked.

"Because she is. You can tell it to look at her, those droopy eyelids and pale skin and pale blue eyes and thin, thin, thin for a baby. She's just not healthy."

"She looks like me when I was a baby. Thin and stuff."

"Not a chance. You have black hair and black eyes and yellow-brown skin. You couldn't have looked any more like her than a cocker spaniel." She shook her head. "You're a little crazy about babies," she said. "All they are is puppies waiting to be grown up and no better as grown-ups than a dog. At least that's the way I see it."

I don't know what I was after with Rosie, but I do know how it felt: a deep hollow in my stomach, an urgency to hold her in my arms so tight she'd melt into me and, in some strange process of osmosis, I'd absorb her.

I thought to tell Paisley Jean about this feeling because it was troubling to me, but I said nothing. I told her goodbye and said I was going to get dressed for Thanksgiving in Georgia Hall, but instead I went down the corridor to the isolation rooms, where I assumed Rosie had been taken.

The doctor on call was coming out of one of the rooms and I wheeled toward him and he put his hand on my wheelchair and turned me around.

"Off-limits," he said.

"I wanted to know about the baby," I said.

"She's sick, but she'll get well, and when she does, you can go back to the ward to visit her."

"It's kind of sad, her being sick on Thanksgiving," I said, with more emotion than I thought I had about it.

"Don't worry," he said. "She doesn't know the difference."

I started to push the elevator's up button, and when the doors opened, he got in with me.

"So you like the babies," he said.

I nodded.

"The nurses have told me about you."

"Maybe because of the babies," I said, pleased to have been noticed.

"You seem to get around more than most of the patients here, and you've developed something of a reputation. Joey Buckley, in the Boys' Ward, had a post-op infection that I took care of, and he asked me did I know you. And now I do."

"What did he tell you?"

"He said that you two are friends."

"We are," I said, and I was probably blushing.

When we got out of the elevator, he smiled and tousled my hair and headed toward the Boys' Ward.

Caroline was gone when I got to the room to dress. Miss Riley stuck her head in the door to say that we'd be leaving in fifteen minutes for Georgia Hall in a caravan of stretchers and wheelchairs, the way we went to the Saturday movies, and I should be dressed soon and ready to line up.

This was an occasion.

I had several dresses in my closet. I actually wore dresses a lot, because they were easier to put on with a cast and more comfortable for sitting in a wheelchair.

My favorite was a red-checked one with long sleeves and white starchy cuffs and a high white collar, a little like a Sister of Mercy, which appealed to me. My mother had made this dress especially for Warm Springs: the skirt was long and full and came to my ankles and covered my cast.

I put the dress on and took out the Alabama baseball cap Joey had given me and went toward the nurses' station, hoping that those of us in wheelchairs would be at the front of the line and, more important, that I might meet Joey coming out of the Boys' Ward.

Miss Riley suggested I take off my baseball cap for Thanksgiving dinner, but I said I couldn't. It was a gift from a friend, another polio, and I might see that person at the dinner.

"But you're going to be at the president's party, remember?" Miss Riley said. "You might want to look your fanciest."

I took off the Alabama cap and put it in my lap.

Dinner was in the late afternoon, probably around five, and it was dark at that hour in November as the wheelchairs and stretchers wound their way to Georgia Hall and the large dining room where we would be celebrating at President Roosevelt's party. There was a sense of family among us, a colony of outsiders whose lives were dignified by kinship to a man like us who had been president of the United States. Everybody, maybe everybody in the world, knew who he was.

It was my first consciousness of value by association, and I was aware that evening of a kind of glamour, as if I were illuminated in the darkness, seen by my friends and enemies at Sidwell Friends and in my neighborhood as I made my way in the long, long line of us to Georgia Hall.

My mother, who I knew was beautiful, told me that I would be beautiful as well when I grew up, and although I was certain that wasn't true, I could believe it was a possibility that Thanksgiving night.

There's a common personality recognized, written about, even filmed, among polio patients — I see it in myself, in others I've known, and in my reading about Roosevelt. It's difficult to know, of course, where nature stops and circumstance takes over. What everyone I knew at Warm Springs certainly shared was a drive to excel, a refusal to quit in the face of extraordinary odds, a determination to go forward and never look back, and a lack of evident self-pity.

Which is not to say that many of us didn't struggle with depression or anger at our dependency — and so, on record, did the president. Roosevelt's experience reflected that of so many polios. He was determined to live as if he were not a cripple, for political reasons — if the electorate saw him as physically disabled, it was thought, they would not believe in his strength to run the country — and for personal reasons as well. Politically, it took enormous effort to present himself as strong and able-bodied: to walk with a cane and locked braces, gripping the arm of whichever strong man stood beside him, usually his son James; to be lifted out of the wheelchair, away from public view; to live a life of "splendid deception."

There is another similarity among polios that struck me in reading about Roosevelt. He was a loner but couldn't bear to be alone, was warm, outgoing, engaging but friendless, sharing little of himself with others, not grief and not frustration, simply putting forth the illusion of cheeriness and ease and fearlessness.

It was a fine cover for a man whose body no longer belonged to him, and I venture that for polios in general, the desire for control stretches far beyond the definition of normal.

I was at the end of the line of girls who lived in the Girls' Ward, and I couldn't find Joey Buckley until we were inside Georgia Hall, and there he was in his wheelchair, separate from the others from the Boys' Ward.

I put on my Alabama cap.

"I think we can sit anyplace we like," I said, wheeling over to him.

"Then you can sit with me and some of the guys," he said. "I was supposed to go home for Thanksgiving."

"Me too," I said.

"My dad got sick and didn't feel well enough to come get me, and my grandma who lives with us doesn't drive on highways."

"I couldn't leave because my stabilization hasn't healed."

We followed the crowd into the large room, candlelit tables with white tablecloths set in a U. On one side of the U were the patients on stretchers, pushed up to the table on their stomachs so they could eat. And on the other side of the U were the wheelchairs. There were no regular chairs at all, no need for a chair except at the far end of the table, the half-circle of the U, an empty chair where Roosevelt would have sat had he been there.

"It's better than Thanksgiving at my grandma's," Joey said to me after grace was spoken, as the plates were served to us. "Like a festival, all us guys together."

"I'm glad I'm here too," I said.

In a far corner of the room, a man stood up, tapped his glass, then every one of us tapped our glasses, and the man called out in a booming voice for us to lift our glasses, and we did, our milk or water or coffee — maybe there was wine, I wouldn't have remembered — in a toast to the head of the table, President Franklin Delano Roosevelt.

"Thank you, Mr. President," we cheered in unison, and then there was the clicking of forks and the chatter of voices and happy laughter.

We could have been anywhere on earth where there was a party.

I See the Moon
and the Moon Sees Me

I WAS WALKING DOWN Macomb Street toward home in September of 1952, after I had left Warm Springs for good and was attending seventh grade at Alice Deal Junior High School. The brick sidewalks on Macomb Street were uneven and mossy, so walking was difficult for me. I did it slowly and in the company of a changing series of characters with whom I'd be engaged in conversation — sometimes the characters were real although not present, sometimes imagined. On that day I was conscious of being both an observer and a participant. I was being watched.

Coming up the street in my direction, toward Wisconsin Avenue, was a young beautiful woman with a Rita Hayworth look, tall, raven-haired, elegant but blowzy — I'd seen that look in movies at Warm Springs. She was wearing a boxy camelhair coat, too big for her and heavy for the climate, and she was smoking a cigarette.

That much I believe was true.

In the time it took us to intersect, at the corner of 36th Street and Macomb, she was pregnant with the child of someone well known in the government, but she was married to another man, so the pregnancy was a secret. She lived downtown near the well-known man but was in our neighborhood to see a doctor, an obstetrician called Dr. Incas, who lived on the next street over. He would perform an abortion in the privacy of his basement office. This was years before *Roe v. Wade*. She could die.

All of this occurred to me as I passed her, headed toward 35th Street and my house. I turned back once and saw that she had stopped, dropped the cigarette on the bricks, and was grinding it out with the toe of her high-heeled shoe.

At dinner that night — dinners were special occasions, evenings I prepared for if my father was going to be at home — I arranged my story. In my small family there was high currency for stories, and on that autumn afternoon I became aware of the process I had followed from the fact of a pretty woman whose coat didn't fit to the fiction of a pregnant beauty on her way to an abortionist.

When I was very young, particularly when I was sick in bed, I'd play with paper dolls with my mother when the soap operas came on. We'd choose our characters before a program began, dress them in their paper clothes for the day, and as the music for, say, *Stella Dallas* rolled out of the console radio, we'd take our places on the bed. In between those hours with my mother when I was four, and seventh grade when I was thirteen and in the real world of junior high, fixed on my chances for election to the cheerleading squad, I was becoming a storyteller.

Reality hovered around my daily life like a fog, and when the air became impossibly thick and close and I couldn't see how to escape it, I discovered a way out.

Warm Springs became for me a festering swamp of hidden possibilities. Hours of time to linger in my own mind and a kind of noisy silence around me, in which I was like a girl on a subway train traveling with strangers. There was no one for whom I was *the* object of affection and so I had no emotional responsibilities. I became someone I could count on. A variety of someones. I filled the time. I don't remember boredom. I could play many parts.

It is true that the story I have told so far in this book doesn't reflect the character of a solitary child lost in her own meanderings.

Rather, one who might, in the language of contemporary psychology, act out.

I was both. Given a choice, I probably would have wanted to be *someone* in the real world, but under the circumstances it wasn't always possible. And so I discovered a way to create a place real enough to me to believe in as fact.

The week after Thanksgiving, I took my Survival Notebook to catechism class.

Some afternoons — and afternoons at Warm Springs could be very long — I'd write a story in my notebook. It would often start with a real story, such as the one my mother loved to tell about the night my father came home late and I was crying and he told my mother he was going to throw me out of the window because I cried too much and replace me the following morning with a teenage boy.

I was never very fond of that story, told off and on throughout my childhood, usually at dinner. In my notebook, I had jotted down the notes for a rewrite:

> Story Outline: Father comes home from the bar a little drunk. Baby is screaming in her crib. He picks her up and throws her out the window. Mid-fall, she turns into a beautiful young girl with wings, and taking flight, she disappears, only to return months later with a wagon full of gifts for the distraught father, beside himself with sadness and remorse. They all lived happily ever after.

"I'm always in trouble," I said, handing Father James the notebook. He glanced at it, skipping over the self-improvement lists, stopping at the stories.

"What is this about?" he asked.

"I rewrite real stories so they come out better."

"I see," he said, closing the notebook. "And what do you want from me?"

I wanted to be excused or absolved of whatever weighed on my mind under the general heading of trouble.

"Never mind," I wanted for him to say after I confessed the problems I had caused. "Do better next time."

That was my understanding of confession. I loved the idea of it, the vision I had of confessing.

I'd slip inside a little box, pull the curtain so I couldn't be seen as a sinner by the public, fall to my knees, press my palms flat against each other in an attitude of prayer. A tiny door would open and I would be able to see the mouth, maybe the nose and eyes — I wasn't sure how much of the face of the priest would show.

But as compelling as confession was to me, I had a problem with forgiveness as I understood it in the Catholic Church. It was too simple that a litany of prayers could liberate a burdened soul like mine from guilt.

I think about guilt now, at an age when it's useful to get rid of things so as not to lug around more than I can carry.

That December afternoon at Warm Springs, I wanted something from Father James. Perhaps relief from my responsibility for bringing unhappiness to the people I loved.

For as long as I could remember, I had been told that my father had hoped to take the job that Edward R. Murrow had been given, broadcasting from Europe during the Second World War.

It was just the kind of assignment my father would have loved. He was twenty-seven years old, longing to be part of the war, rejected as a soldier for having flat feet. The story my parents told was that he had turned down the offer because I was too ill for him to go to London, and so Murrow got the job. It was evident by the way my mother spent her time that she had given up her life for me. And my brother had given up his mother to me.

Those were the repeated chords of my childhood. Or so I imagined. I don't know whether they were actually repeated by my parents or told to me only once and so deeply affected me, or even whether nothing was said directly to me at all, but were instead stories I overheard, always listening to overhear.

Suffice to say I defined myself as being *too much trouble*. Somehow in those early years that perception got woven into the fabric of who I was, how I was seen by others, how I perceived myself. Caught up in the dilemma of the sick child, the center of attention, I was an inadvertent troublemaker, an albatross around the family's neck.

My situation was like a recurring attack of hives. Something must be terribly wrong if every time I arrived at a new place — and I loved the opportunity promised by arrivals — something went haywire. I was emotionally klutzy, like a person who walks into a room and knocks the crystal off the tables, but the stakes in my "accidents" were higher than the loss of cut glass.

I had a sense of failure and importance scrambled in a single bowl.

This sounds far weightier than it was, and I look back on my childhood as being more happy than unhappy. But like most storytellers, I write to make sense of the disorder in our lives.

Happiness is a mirage, a phantom hope that seeps into the spirit, taking us by surprise. What counts over the long haul is the pursuit of happiness.

What I must have been hoping to find with Father James was my own self.

I wanted to get rid of my habit of bursting out of the starting gate before the gun, my tendency to live life by accident, as if there were not always some intention beyond carelessness. I wanted to compensate for the problems I caused to the people I loved, or start over from the beginning, or make up a new beginning with a different set of inevitabilities.

Father James was reading when I came into the room, and he looked up over his glasses.

He had the kind of pale, elegant face that registered expression only in the eyes and otherwise maintained a preternatural calm. That day I was expecting nothing from him but the usual lesson and, after I showed him my notebook, a gentle conversation and an interest in what I had to say.

But he had a different subject in mind.

"What happened with Magnolia?" he asked.

"What do you mean?"

"I understand something happened with Magnolia."

"She's the little girl who stays in the supply room while her mother mops the floors," I said. "She's my friend."

"She bit a child in the Children's Ward."

I took the notebook I had brought to show him and slid it between an arm of my wheelchair and my hip.

"Why did you take her into the Children's Ward?" he asked.

"I took her in to see the babies. She has nothing to do all day," I said. "No one told me I shouldn't."

"Well, they should have told you. They should have told you that Magnolia was to be left alone at her mother's request and that you are allowed in the Children's Ward only as a special privilege."

"She bit Violet Blue by accident, not on purpose. She's deaf. You can't tell her things she can or cannot do."

His chin rested on his fist, and he was looking not at me but just beyond, at the closed door behind us, and probably thinking he wished he didn't have to have this conversation.

I wonder now how Father James got to Warm Springs in the first place, and what he was doing spending so much time with me. Did he actually believe he had a new soul to deliver into the hands of God? Was I really interesting to him, or was he just lonely, like me, without his countrymen or his own church or his wife, whom he had left or who had died?

Race in the United States must have been perplexing to him, and I myself didn't understand at the time what it was that separated Magnolia and me. Only that something did.

"You ask for trouble," Father James said, opening the catechism book to the day's lesson, reading it to himself as if he didn't know it already by heart. "Why ask for trouble? is my question to you. Why do you need problems when you have enough? Everyone here has enough problems not to go looking for new ones."

I started to answer, but he shook his head.

"Don't talk," he said. "I asked you a question that you should think about for a long time. Maybe even years."

Paisley Jean had been the one to tell, the only one who knew to tell, since Magnolia couldn't have told even her mother. She told me she was sorry to have gotten me into trouble, that Violet Blue's finger did get infected and then she couldn't "lie" about it, and she did say that I had come with Magnolia to the Children's Ward but the biting was not my fault, or Magnolia's, but her own.

I was impressed by Paisley Jean's honesty. Grown-ups, in my brief experience, did not often take the blame for things.

"So that's over, and not to worry, but I've got bad news," Paisley Jean said, pulling me down on the chair so I was sitting next to her. "Rosie has polio."

"But she's had polio already," I said.

"Well, she's got it again."

"Is this a secret?" I asked.

"It won't be a secret for long," Paisley Jean replied.

I left the Children's Ward, pushed the up button, and went back to my room, where Caroline was just finishing her lesson with Miss Forkman.

"Guess what?" I said after Miss Forkman left. "One of the babies in the Children's Ward has polio again."

"That's not possible," Caroline said with her usual confidence. "You can only get it once."

"Well, Rosie has it and she's already had it once." I didn't add about Rosie's mother, because Caroline didn't like what she called my *blown-up* stories, whether they were true or not.

"Maybe you better shut our door," Caroline said, and I wheeled over and shut it.

"Should we ask Dr. Iler?" I wondered.

Caroline nodded.

"You ask," I said. "He thinks you're more serious than me."
What I really thought but could not have articulated at the time
was that Caroline had the *right* to ask whether the polio virus was
floating around Warm Springs because she was severely handicapped, and I did not have that right.

Caroline said, "I thought you only got polio once and you were
sick for about a month and when you started to get well some of
your muscles were okay and some were not, depending on how
sick you'd been. But at least after it was gone, you were immune to
getting it again."

"That's what I thought too," I said.

A year and a half later, in 1952, Jonas Salk announced his discovery
of the vaccine against polio, during a nationwide epidemic affect-
ing more than forty-five thousand people.

Most of us, certainly as children, did not know very much
about the disease we'd had. The main problem for polios was to
persuade others that although the effects of polio remained, the
disease had gone. We were not contagious. That's all I knew. I'd
said it often, from the time I was little, to anyone who questioned
my health or looked at me askance.

"I'm not catching," I'd say, sensing others' fear of me.

"I think we need to keep the door closed all the time," Caroline said, "and maybe we shouldn't eat the food. It could carry
germs."

"What'll we eat?" I asked, inclined in any case to turn up the
heat to the level of emergency.

"You can get us dinner at the candy store. Crackers and stuff,
and hide it in your sweater drawer."

"Are you going to tell your parents?" I asked. "I don't think I
will."

"They'll worry too much," Caroline agreed. "I won't either."

We skipped lunch that day, without Miss Riley's interference, but at dinner, when our trays went back untouched, the night nurse, Miss Barnes, came in to ask what was the matter.

"I have a note you skipped lunch," she said.

"We're not hungry," Caroline said.

"You'll be very hungry. I'm bringing back your trays."

Caroline said she didn't feel well. I said we were both sick, probably with the stomach flu.

"I'm bringing back the trays anyway," Miss Barnes said.

"The food is sure to have germs, since it's been sitting out in the hall with all the other finished trays," Caroline said. "I'm eating nothing that isn't in a package."

When Miss Barnes returned, we ate the packaged saltines and drank milk from the carton but left the rest, although I couldn't keep myself from eating the chocolate pudding.

I had picked up Ritz crackers and a jar of peanut butter and two Cokes at the candy store, and we ate the whole box of crackers and the peanut butter.

I wanted to find Rosie. I'd stand at the door of her room and check if she was breathing.

Caroline took the situation of Rosie's polio very seriously.

"You can't come back into this room if you get exposed to her," she said.

At lights out, when Miss Barnes came in with laxatives and juice, Caroline asked her how the child with polio was doing.

"There is no child with polio in the hospital — if what you mean by polio is active illness. You all *had* polio, of course."

We nodded.

"I *know* there is a child with polio," I said.

"Who told you?"

"A nurse," I said. "I don't know her name."

"Maybe you can point her out to me," she said.

"I can't," I said.

"Or won't," Miss Barnes said coolly.

"I won't," I said, glad to protect Paisley Jean as she had protected me.

"Well . . ." Miss Barnes started to say something, but she changed her mind and left the room, so distracted she forgot her tray of laxatives.

"What do you think?" I asked.

"I think they want to keep it a secret because it'll be a mess if we get a polio epidemic at a polio hospital," Caroline said. "Maybe I *should* call my parents."

"Maybe you should."

But I was not going to call mine. I didn't want them to worry, and at the time I didn't want them to come to Warm Springs. It was my plan to return home to them without flaw or fault. They would be giddy with happiness to see the changes I'd made.

After lights out, I lay on my back with my eyes open, aching for Rosie. Across the room, Caroline was on her stomach, her face resting in her fists. She was wide awake. The light from the moon slid over her face, and she was lovely and vulnerable in that light, and at that moment I believed I loved her.

I wondered what it must be like to be confined to bed while germs too small to see were spreading through the air around you and you couldn't move without help.

Caroline never spoke about her life with polio, had never mentioned what it had been like to walk and then not walk ever again, how it had felt when she got sick.

But that night she told me some things. About the way her friends had been with her, curious at first, anxious to see what polio looked like on a girl they'd known, and then too busy to take the time to go to her house after school. About the loneliness of home-schooling and how someday she was going to be a lawyer for poor people who needed her, and she'd go live by herself in a first-floor apartment in case there was a fire.

"What if we had a fire here?" she asked.

"They'd get us out."

"There're so many of us, more than they have people to get us out." And then she added, "You could get us out."

"I could get you out."

"How could you do it with me in this cast?"

"I just could," I said.

We stayed up all night, watching the sun rise deep yellow over the trees, and I told Caroline things I had never told anyone, things I scarcely thought about or remembered until I started to talk about myself. I was unaccustomed to personal narrative except with my mother.

I used to think concealment was a virtue, and since I believed myself to be short on virtues, I was glad to count on that one. People told me their lives — girls my age, older girls, boys, grown-ups, people of all ages whom I knew or ran into on streetcars or in bookstores or libraries — and I listened. I was glad to have their lives — it gave me a sense of accumulating friendships. But I kept my own life under wraps. I imagine that Caroline was similar, and spoke to me that night only because it was night and we were vaguely afraid of what might be happening at Warm Springs with Rosie's polio and whether it could happen to us.

At one point in the middle of the night, as I faded in and out of sleep, Caroline raised her voice.

"Please don't fall asleep," she said.

I said I wouldn't, but I did fall asleep, and she woke me again, this time in a voice near panic.

"I need you not to sleep!" she said.

Then, to my own surprise, because it was both personal and revealing, I told her about the promises I used to exact from my parents every night — *promise not this and promise not that* until my stiff, worried body finally relaxed into the mattress and I fell asleep.

Caroline was quiet for a long time, so I was primed for one

of her acerbic remarks, expecting it. But instead she spoke in a voice more pensive and tentative than I was familiar with from her.

"We need to keep ourselves a secret."

I read a lot of fiction, but only occasionally do I read something that hits home so powerfully that I'm left with the full memory of that first reading. "Good Country People" by Flannery O'Connor was one of those stories. I was in my first year of graduate school, sitting up in bed, alternately reading and listening for the waking calls of my first son, and I remember the emotional shock as I reached the end of the story.

In the story, a young woman with a wooden leg is visited by a traveling Bible salesman, who persuades her to let him come up to her secret hideaway and then prevails on her to take off her wooden leg. He leaves with the leg, and she is trapped in her hideaway and humiliated. I was physically sickened by the story and so disturbed when I finished it that I took a shower and stood under the spray weeping, the water running so my little boy wouldn't hear me crying.

When my children, especially my daughters, were young, I warned them against trusting easily. It saddens me that I had children before I knew enough about myself to shield them from my own suspicions. They didn't need my childhood in addition to their own.

"Don't show too much," I'd say to them. "Don't let anyone know that you feel helpless."

Recently, my younger son was working in Japan with the Special Olympics. He told me that some Japanese, although pleased from a political and economic point of view to host the event, wanted the crippled athletes to be invisible. They would bring bad press if allowed to move freely and mingle with the public.

And not many years ago, I was standing at a window with one of my colleagues at George Mason University as a work crew was putting in ramps and bars and automatic doors for the handi-capped.

"Why do we need this stuff?" the colleague asked. "These peo-ple should stay at home."

I don't think it even crossed his mind that I was one of *these people.*

Dr. Stern, who was the head of surgery, arrived at our room early the next morning, just at dawn, in scrubs.

He took a seat between Caroline's bed and mine.

"What's this I hear about a child with polio at Warm Springs?"

"That's what I was told," I said. "I was told that a baby called Cynthia — I call her Rosie — is in isolation with polio again."

"That's true," he said. "She has been diagnosed with nonpara-lytic polio. But it's unlikely — not impossible but very unlikely — that anyone here will get it."

And then he told us about polio, what it is and how it is spread. I had never asked my parents or any doctor about the disease it-self, never wanted to know, but Dr. Stern's scientific explanation gave a specific identity to our lives. The doctor was in our room for half an hour, maybe less, but it was the first time I had been taken so seriously, the first time I had been spoken to by anyone besides my parents who assumed I was capable of understanding the complexities.

"So we're polios," I said to Caroline after Dr. Stern had left. "That's just who we are."

"Like a club, and no one else but us can belong."

We laughed, laughed and giggled for a long time, near tears with relief. We were conspirators, finally recognizing each other as residents of the same hometown, where we'd been living as if sep-arated by miles instead of by an air space of three feet.

When I first arrived in the room I was going to share with Caro-line Slover, I noticed that she took exception. I thought she was contemptuous of my stronger body, and perhaps she was. I hadn't earned my place at Warm Springs.

Implicit in our relationship was her fear of dependency and what my arrival as her roommate might mean to her, so we skirted each other's tiny territory. I misunderstood her reserve as a judgment and we never spoke of it. She was independent of help or sympathy. I should have realized that however long it took her to move from one place to another, she would do it alone. The same instinct was deep in the fabric of my own character.

I was a kind of steward, custodial in my friendships. There is a photograph of me walking before I contracted polio, so I had only just learned to walk, and my head is turned back toward a little girl behind me who is dragging a wagon. My hand reaches out to her. My mother used to show me that picture as an example of my sweet and generous nature. But then again, she was my mother.

Whether I would have been that same child without polio, who's to say? But caretaking became a safety net for me as I negotiated the life of a normal, healthy child, gravitating to those who were frail or needy or lonely or simply, like me, outsiders.

If I made myself indispensable, then I would never be left alone.

To be left alone was my great fear, but at that time I would not have believed it. I thought of myself as invincible of spirit, which is how my mother saw me. And it is possible that her belief was a bridge to my own eventual hard-won belief that I might, just might, survive without her.

In character studies of Franklin Roosevelt, much is made of his isolation and reserve, his refusal to become preoccupied with problems, his insistence on optimism, his loneliness. In everything I've read, Roosevelt was warm and engaging before the public and restrained in his intimate relationships.

He was, especially after he had polio, always surrounded by people, both by necessity and by choice. Yet his various biographers would argue that in spirit he was always alone.

Although such a description of character speaks to his aristo-cratic upbringing and his position as an only child, to the climate of the times and his particular construct of a warm and gregari-ous personality, it also reflects the problems of dependency and how they arrange themselves to protect a person's vulnerability.

When my youngest child, Kate, was nine or ten, her choral group planned to sing a Japanese children's song at an event at the Kennedy Center, sponsored by the Japanese embassy.

"I can't do it," she said the night before the event was to take place. "People will see my mistakes."

"How many children in your chorus?" I asked.

"Maybe a hundred."

"You won't make a mistake," I said, "but even if you were to do so, how would anyone know with so many people onstage?"

"*I* would know," she said.

Kate was born when I was five and a half months pregnant. She was tiny, fragile, sickly, and we hovered over her, rushed her to emergency rooms, stayed up all night, ever watchful, my eyes glued to her every breath. I was a nervous, smothering, ensnaring terrier of a mother with her, and it was no wonder that she was afraid she'd be visible in a chorus of a hundred children.

I too would have imagined that I was being watched, not for my failures, as worried Kate, but for my imagined and various successes.

When I retrieved my first novel, the one I had written five years after I left Warm Springs, I had forgotten the story. It had been more than forty years since I had written it, and I'd never looked at it again after I graduated from college. I wanted to read it this time for the context, certain that there would be many particulars in that story on which I could count for this one, places and peo-ple and the look and feel of things, including myself, things I cer-tainly had forgotten. And I was right.

I recognized a memory of myself and my parents and Caroline

and others, what I did every day, how I assembled a life with other people — much made of little, in that story as in this one.

I have never forgotten the end of my time at Warm Springs. As I was reading along in *Wooden and Wicker,* prepared for the inevitability of the last chapter, I was stunned to discover that in the novel I had changed the single significant event of my years at Warm Springs to suit my desire for a different conclusion.

When I was eight, I was given a set of opera librettos by my aunt Elsie. I loved the high drama of the stories and decided to put them on in our living room for my parents and some of the neighbors — without the music, of course. I did no rewriting of the librettos except for the final acts, which usually concluded in disaster, with the characters dying or disappearing or left in some state of despair.

I crossed out the last page of each set of librettos, and in its place I wrote: "And they all lived happily ever after."

III

Dress Rehearsal

The Art of the Positive

IN LATE JUNE OF 1951, after spending six months at home, I was to return to Warm Springs for a final year, during which I would have muscle transplants. The stabilization that was the first stage of surgery was successful and I had gone home for Christmas. So had Joey Buckley.

"I won't be back until summer," he said. "The stabilizations are going to have to heal before they can do any more surgery."

I was stunned with sadness. For days after he left, I sat in my wheelchair outside the candy store eating Clark bars.

That Christmas, my parents had photographs taken of Jeffrey and me in our ordinary lives, as if our lives were ordinary. I had returned from Warm Springs in worse shape than I'd been in when I arrived. I was in braces, on crutches, in orthopedic shoes with a three-and-a-half-inch lift, and the Clark bars had taken effect.

There are pictures of us in front of John Eaton Elementary School and the Congregational church, which was the closest church to our house, although we had almost never attended it; in front of Alice Deal Junior High, where I would go when I finally returned from Warm Springs; on our front steps; on the swings at the Macomb Street playground across the street; with General Beauregard in the back yard — posed photographs of a life we didn't lead, Jeffie and I dressed in appropriate outfits for the recorded occasions.

It was so unlike my parents to send out photographs of their children to relatives in Ohio and Michigan, to the friends with whom they'd grown up, as if we were a normal American family. It was as though they were somehow ashamed and wanted to prove to others that we *were* normal now, finally, at Christmas 1950, and that we were all well and happy at school, in church, cavorting with our dog in the back yard.

We were odd. We would have been odd if I hadn't had polio, if Jeffie hadn't been dead terrified of school, if Grandma Richards had been a regular grandma and let her boobs go the way of all flesh instead of buying new ones at the five-and-ten, if my father had asked the drunks to sleep in their own houses, if he'd left the stray cats and dogs on the streets and given up civil rights as a personal war in a segregated city.

I wanted to go back to Warm Springs. I had planned a triumphant return to Washington and this first visit was a fiasco, a complete failure, but I kept it to myself.

When my mother asked why I didn't want to see my friends at home, I told her that I wanted to stay around the house with the family. And that was true. Even when Harold Ickes called to invite me to the farm, I told him I wasn't allowed.

The plan was that I'd return to Warm Springs for muscle transplant surgery and then physical therapy through the winter and return home again in late spring, to spend a month at the end of sixth grade at John Eaton Elementary. I'd then travel back again in June with my mother for a last series of surgeries.

My mother would not travel by herself. She was able to drive with a child in the car, so it wasn't the actual driving that frightened her. It was driving alone. I wasn't aware of this phobia until that June, when I was disappointed to learn that my grandmother Lindsey Greene, my mother's stepmother, whom I disliked more intensely than I have ever disliked anyone in my life, would be coming with us.

I should have sensed something fragile about my mother, but we lived in a kind of maze, a finely spun fairy tale created by my parents in which some things were clear and some were fuzzy, but the general tone of our lives together as a family gave the impression of honesty and closeness, and so I assumed that what I saw was true. I didn't realize until I was older that seeing is a matter of choice.

Sometime after I was eight and had been healthy for maybe as long as a year, my mother retreated to her room. She did it gracefully, as if it were a plan she'd had in order to accomplish something I was too young to understand, as if it wouldn't have interested me in any case. For almost a year, until I was preparing to go to Warm Springs, she lived in her room. We lived there, off and on, with her — General Beauregard and Jeffie and I and Grandma Richards. Often my aunt Janet, who was my mother's cousin by her father's second marriage, was there, and my father too, when he got home from work. He had their bedroom door replaced with a Dutch door, the top half of which was kept open onto the hall so my mother could hear what was going on in the house without having to leave her room. We ate dinner in my parents' bedroom, and after dinner we played games. It was cheerful and I loved coming home from school knowing exactly where to find her.

Nothing ever got said about the obvious, that it was unusual for a mother to spend all of her time in her bedroom. And so, it became the way we lived.

I didn't mention it to my friends. And I wasn't much interested in inviting them over to play.

Once a week, I'd go with her in the afternoon to Dr. April, who was an asthma doctor. A taxi would pick us up, since my mother was no longer driving. I'd go up in the elevator and sit in the waiting room while she got shots from Dr. April and they talked. Usually it took an hour, and then we'd go home by taxi and I'd follow her up to her bedroom, where she'd go to bed.

The shots, she said, exhausted her.

"Do you have asthma?" I once asked her.

"No," she said. "I don't."

*   *   *

One day, she came out of her room, went downstairs, put a leash on General Beauregard, and took him for a walk. And that night we had dinner in the dining room.

We did not discuss the year we lived in my parents' bedroom until years later, when I was in my early twenties and married. My father was dead by then, and I had started to have debilitating panic attacks.

"I think I'm losing my mind," I told my mother.

"I promise you're not losing your mind," she said, echoing the language that hushed my childhood fears. "They used to call this condition a nervous breakdown."

And that was that.

Lindsey Greene caused my mother great unhappiness. According to family legend, easy to believe, my grandfather married Lindsey, a maiden lady fifteen years older than my mother whose fiancé had been killed in the First World War, under duress. Urbana was a small, incestuous town, and he had a young daughter with whom, by Urbana standards, he should not have been living in a rooming house alone. When he died in an accident at his mill, not long after they were married, my mother was left alone with Lindsey's rage and mercurial temper.

One night when I was six and Jeffie a baby and we were living in Georgetown, I got up the courage to tell my mother that I didn't like her mother very much.

My mother was leaning on the door of my bedroom, lovely and mysterious in the diffused light from the hall.

"You don't have to like her, darling," she said, and then, in a voice wistful and sweet and so very quiet I could barely hear her: "I had a real mother once."

We drove to Urbana: eight hours across Maryland, to the Pennsylvania Turnpike, into West Virginia and then Ohio. I loved being in a car alone with my mother, or a train or a boat, and we went places together, just the two of us, even after I was married. I don't know what we talked about, but we always talked and talked. About her past, about my future. She listened on these trips as if there were no one in her life who held so much fascination for her.

The house in Urbana where my mother had lived with Lindsey Greene — where her father had died and where she had married my father — was Lindsey's house, but it had been left by my grandfather to my mother. This particular point was made clear to me when I was very young, and what it meant, as far as I was concerned, was that the house where Lindsey lived belonged to our family with Grandma Richards and General Beauregard. It wouldn't have been an issue for a girl except for the fact that my father wasn't allowed to spend the night at what we called 222 College Street, in order to avoid calling it Lindsey Greene's.

I was probably six or seven when I saw the nature of my mother's relationship with Lindsey, but it was a long time before I understood it, not in fact until Lindsey died in 2002, years after my mother's death.

We went to Urbana for a couple of weeks every summer, usually my mother and Jeffie and I, but on one trip my father came along. A few streets away, Grandma Richards, who spent her summers in Urbana to be close to whoever remained of her eleven brothers and sisters, lived in an apartment, one big room with a kitchen and a toilet, separated from the kitchen by a curtain — a bed-sitter, she called it, on the third floor of someone's house on Scioto Street.

We had driven from Washington, the luggage was still in the car, and we were having dinner at Lindsey's — we called her Nana to her face.

At the end of dinner, Lindsey got up from the table — she was a small woman, not unattractive, with Irish freckled skin and short curly hair and a figure more virginal than mature — and asked my father to bring in my mother's and Jeffie's and my bags.

It was the first time in my conscious memory that we had all been in Urbana together. Although I knew that Lindsey didn't approve of my father, I had never seen evidence of it.

I asked where my father would be staying.

"At Grandma Richards's," my mother said.

"I'm going with Daddy," I said.

"Me too," Jeffie said.

My father brought in my mother's luggage and took it up to the room in which she had slept as a young girl. He kissed her goodnight on the large Victorian front porch under the porch light, took Jeffie's and my hand, and off we went in the old faithful lavender Chevrolet.

The last image I had that night was of my mother standing alone under the porch light, waving to the back of our car.

"Lindsey Greene's got airs," Grandma Richards said as my brother and I snuggled into bed with her, my father sleeping on the couch in the same room. "And no one who lives in Urbana, Ohio, should have a right to airs."

Lindsey was already packed when we arrived at 222 College Street for the drive to Warm Springs.

"I don't like the heat," she said, maybe the first thing she said when we arrived, before she even said hello. She smelled of dead gardenias, and if her own mother, whom I called Gammie, were not always baking sugar cookies and pies and cakes when we visited, the house would have smelled of dead gardenias too.

"It won't be too hot in June," my mother said.

I'm sure she was bracing for the long trip south with Lindsey, not an easy trade-off for her fear of driving alone.

I slept in the twin bed in my mother's bedroom at the house in Urbana, and I loved to sleep there because my mother had when she was my age. Before we turned out the lights, my mother reading to me while I half slept on my back, Lindsey looked in the doorway.

"I can't stand the heat. You know that, Betty."

"I do know that," my mother said, repeating, "but it won't be too hot in June."

Caroline was still in our old room on Second Medical, but a girl called Annabelle, a silent, sullen girl who stared out the window when I walked into the room, was living there in my place. I was put in the Girls' Ward instead, in one of the beds lined up against three walls, amid a constant din of voices, which at night ran down slowly like an old car engine until the ward finally quieted.

Lindsey came with my mother while I was readmitted to the hospital. She sat in a chair leafing through a magazine, but when I was called to go upstairs, she told my mother she'd meet her at the hotel. She didn't like hospitals, she said. She was feeling nauseated.

"It's quite unsanitary here, isn't it," she said as the elevator doors opened to take my mother and me up to the Girls' Ward on the second floor.

"Is it?" I asked my mother in the elevator.

"Of course not," my mother said. "It's a hospital. It has to be kept clean."

She never disagreed with Lindsey when in her presence, not that I remember.

Miss Riley greeted us when the elevator doors opened. She seemed — at least I thought she seemed — genuinely glad to see me.

She told me that some of the babies in the Children's Ward had gone home, but Rosie was still there and doing very well, and Violet Blue would certainly remember me, and Sue Sue and maybe some others.

"Magnolia?" I asked.

"Magnolia's here on Tuesdays and Thursdays. Her mother has a job at the hotel on the other days."

I followed Miss Riley to the Girls' Ward.

"Joey Buckley's back."

My heart leapt.

"Just last week he got back for his second round of surgeries. And Father James is home from seeing his family in Ireland."

I had never told my parents about catechism classes. I don't know what they would have thought about my conversion to Catholicism. Probably very little. They didn't have opinions to put in our way when we were growing up.

I didn't want them to know about Father James, although my mother had met him in passing. But the unspoken story between us had a quality of secrecy and shame. I wouldn't talk about it.

The muscle transplant surgery was scheduled for the end of the first week. My leg and ankle were nothing but bone. I was told to be careful not to twist my ankle, because I could break the stabilization. I needed muscles to be able to walk; otherwise there was nothing in that leg to support the skeleton. It's my understanding that in the first muscle transplant, the shin muscle, which controlled my ability to lift my foot, was moved to serve as a calf muscle and held in place for the several months I was in a cast by wires strung through the muscle and a "rubber button," with holes for the wires located externally on my heel. This surgery was more painful than the stabilization and the re-forming of my foot, and more aggravating. The muscle, urgent to return home, is always straining to get there.

I was to get new muscles in my calf and a small transplant in my big toe, so the toe wouldn't drop and trip me when I was barefoot. This time I would be in Warm Springs for almost a year, with only a month or two at home before another muscle transplant and more weeks of physical therapy.

I liked that I'd be living in the Girls' Ward, liked the thought of a room full of girls, especially at night and after my mother had left. Early on, I had learned to make a place for myself in a crowd, but that afternoon before my surgery, sitting up in bed, bored and nervous and not permitted to eat, I wasn't quite in the mood for making friends with the fifteen girls on the ward, most of whom I'd never seen before.

My bed was the last one next to the door, a placement determined by the order of surgery. Since I was next to be operated on, I'd occupy that bed until another surgical patient took it over, and gradually I'd move around the room as others came up for their operations. We were all engaged in this slow movement of our beds around the rectangular ward. The changing sightlines gave an illusion of adventure to our daily lives. I had either a window opposite my bed or the wall, either Elaine was across from me or Amy or Francy was, a fluid social geography. Tomorrow could always be a social improvement on today.

On one side of me was the door to the corridor and on the other was Sandy Newcombe. I could tell we were going to be friends because she wanted desperately for that to happen.

"So, Susan — is that what you call yourself? Or Sue?" Sandy was in a body cast, leaning over her side table as close to my bed as she could possibly get. "Maybe Sue. I've got a friend named Sue in Waco, Texas, where my folks live, only they call her Sue Bunny. A crazy name, Sue Bunny, but that's Waco for you."

"Susan," I said.

She told me her name and her school and her surgery, the same as Caroline's had been, and this and that, on and on through afternoon snacks and dinner, until my mother came upstairs to be with me. She spoke to Sandy awhile and then closed the curtains between our beds.

My mother sat down in the chair beside me, running her fingers over my arm, and in her soft, musical voice went over the details of the operation as Dr. Iler had described them. She liked the precision of medical conversation, and it was comforting for me to listen to her talk about the muscles, to repeat the scientific names. The gastrocnemius — the name of one of the calf muscles that had atrophied with the rest of the calf muscles and showed no sign of traces — would be replaced with the tibialis anterior, my shin muscle, which had shown some trace of response. The hope was that the shin muscle transplanted to my calf would develop through physical therapy and I would be able to walk normally. The shin muscle, Dr. Iler had explained, wasn't critical for walking. As it turns out, I don't notice its absence, except that I can't move my ankle at all or lift my foot up or push it down.

That night, a feeling of dread, as if it were actual and liquid, filled my chest. I hadn't been nervous before the first surgery: my defenses were no doubt securely in place because they had to be — the ready charm, the easy dismissal of expressions of concern. *I'm fine, perfectly fine.*

I knew this time that the surgery would be painful, and I was braced for it. The dread was about fear, not pain, a lingering fear, and what it brought to mind was the nights of pleading with my parents for promises of safety when I was small. A systemic fear I couldn't articulate.

My mother described the aftermath of surgery — the anxious little tibialis longing to be back where it belonged, the swelling, the inflammation, worse with muscles than with bone. Or so Dr. Iler expected. She didn't even ask if she could come early the next morning to see me before I went downstairs to the waiting room with the iron lung.

"Ask Lindsey to stay in the hotel," I said.

"Don't worry. Lindsey is uncomfortable in hospitals," my mother said, blowing me a kiss. She always left me with a kiss, blown across the air space between us. There were no sentimental good-byes, no tears. We had gone through this scenario many times in our lives together.

That night I couldn't sleep at all, but I kept my eyes closed for Sandy Newcombe, jabbering away in the next bed about how she had been about to play the witch in *The Wizard of Oz,* and on opening night, just as she was going onstage, she got sick and then sicker and by the time she went home that night, she had polio.

"Am I keeping you awake?" she asked.

I didn't answer, but someone called out from across the room, "Please. You're keeping all of us awake."

We were polite to one another in the Girls' Ward.

Sometime during the months at Warm Springs, I had learned

to move pain, as if it were an object, from one part of my body to another. After the stabilization, still sedated, on my back, propped slightly up, the bottom of my bed raised to minimize the throbbing, I found satisfaction imagining that the pain in my ankle was actually in my arm. It was miraculous to be able to move it from one place to another with my mind. By thinking it to my arm, the arm didn't hurt, but if I imagined the pain just above the ankle, I didn't feel it in the ankle either. Like an experiment in chemistry class, mixing this and that and the combination becomes something else altogether. Of course the trick didn't last because pain is pain, but I wasn't entirely at its mercy, and that was something.

Waiting was a condition of our lives, especially during the weeks after surgery. There was nothing to do. We couldn't move or read or watch television or even listen to the radio. There was no entertainment in any case, except Saturday movies or trading cards or books or card games or conversation. In those long weeks of waiting I had hours of white space to fill.

It was similar in discipline to my experience with traces. I knew there was a muscle, say, in my foot, and if I thought "foot," I should be able to contact the messenger and lift the foot. I could even feel its place, but concentrating on moving the muscle did no good. Nothing happened. With a trace there is a little *ping* of recognition, a tiny cry of *I'm here but just barely,* but no movement. It is that *ping* that promises the possibility for a muscle to restore itself.

I filled the white space. I could wait for hours and not be restless if I slipped into the empty pool and made believe it was full.

Years ago, after I'd written the Warm Springs book and decided I wanted to be a writer but was worried that I had nothing to write about, I read an interview with Joyce Carol Oates. When she was asked where she found her material, Oates replied, "In my fantasies." And *vroom*, like a small explosion in the brain, I had stories and stories and stories as a gift from those months of waiting. I was always somewhere else and the narrative took over. I had the illusion of living a life in full.

But that restless night before surgery, I was afraid, not of the surgery itself, but of something else, something I wanted to have and couldn't ask for. I remember the feeling specifically, was aware even at the time it was happening. I turned on the light for the nurse, with the intention of asking her to call my mother at the hotel, but when she arrived, I was embarrassed and asked if I could have a glass of water, knowing I could not.

Maybe, I thought, I wanted my father to be there.

I never remember thinking, Why didn't he come to Warm Springs? I wouldn't have asked him to come, but that night I wished that he were there with my mother, that Lindsey were back in Urbana, and that the following morning my parents would be standing so I could see them through the window of the waiting room, clasping hands.

When my youngest child was small and after her father and I had divorced, she said to me that all she wanted in her whole life was to walk between us, holding our hands.

I must have been sad, but that's retrospective thinking. For years I fought sadness as if it had the power to extinguish my life, and the antidote to its creeping insistence was work.

I couldn't wait until the surgery was done and I was back in my wheelchair, hustling through the corridors with bedpans and mail, brightening the Children's Ward with my urgent attention.

I was slow to wake up from the anesthesia. What I remember hearing was a girl's voice chattering in my ear as if she were right next to my head, blowing down my ear canal.

"You screamed all night," Sandy Newcombe was saying. "I mean these long screams, and we were lying in bed, all of us listening for you to take a breath, and the scream just went on and on."

I looked over at the place where my mother should be, the chair next to my bed, and no one was there, only a sliver of Sandy Newcombe's face straight on me.

"It must hurt something terrible," Sandy said. "Does it hurt a lot?"

I didn't answer.

"We thought you'd died when you didn't take a breath."

I pushed the light for the nurse, and when Miss Riley appeared and I asked for a Coca-Cola, she said I couldn't have one yet. Twenty-four hours, she said.

"What time is it?" I asked.

"Dinnertime," she said. "Smell the chicken?"

The smell of fried chicken was strong and made me ill.

"Do you know where my mother is?"

"She's been here all day since you came up from recovery. She'll be back."

I closed my eyes. I didn't like that I had screamed out without my knowledge, and so I fought to stay awake.

"Pain?" someone asked in my ear.

It was dark, so it must have been late, but not late enough for lights out.

"No pain," I said, which wasn't exactly true. I could feel it coming, marching, marching, the way pain does, starting as a whisper, then louder and louder in a steady crescendo.

"Turn on your light if it hurts."

I nodded.

I wanted to ask about my mother but was worried that if I said her name, said *Where is my mother?*, said *mother* out loud, I would weep.

Later, the ward hushed with girls' whispering, I felt her hand over my forehead, her fingertips on my cheeks.

"Where've you been?" I asked.

She didn't reply. Then she said, "I can tell it hurts."

"A little. Just a little," I said.

"You should take pain medicine if they offer it to you."

"It makes me feel sick," I said.

"Ask for half, then," she whispered.

It was dark and I settled into the safety of her hand brushing over my face, the steady rhythm of it, her soft breathing next to my ear.

"What's going to happen with Lindsey?" I asked.

"She is going to be too hot and complain about it," she said.

"Is it hot? I feel shivery."

"Not too hot," she said.

All night, I could feel my mother's presence while I slept, conscious of her hands running down my arms, stretching my fingers, her fingers lacing through my hair.

In the morning, she was gone.

"Your grandmother called the hospital when it was still dark," Sandy Newcombe said. "Miss Riley came in really early this morning and told your mother that your grandmother had called from the hotel for her to come back because your grandmother was very sick."

"So she left?"

"She left. She told Miss Riley she'd be back soon."

A girl I'd seen before but whose name I didn't know, a big girl with square bangs and long, dark hair and long casts on both legs sticking out in front of her, stopped by my bed.

"You had a bad time last night," she said.

"I was too woozy to feel a bad time," I replied.

"Trust me," the girl said. "You were crying. I was so glad when your mom came back from dinner and settled you down."

She said her name was Jennifer and she was from Florida, on the beach, and her family had a boat.

"So I actually cried?" I asked.

"No kidding," Jennifer said.

"I never cry," I said.

When my mother returned it was still morning, my second day after surgery. She was wearing a straight beige dress with a long skirt, a high mandarin collar, tiny black bead earrings, and high heels. I could hear her coming from the elevator and knew who it was. Only my mother would wear high heels in a hospital.

My mother had outfits for all occasions. Dresses she wore to travel, suits for the afternoon, long skirts and fitted blouses for the evening. I believe that having been stalked by emergencies, she gained a sense of control by dressing in clothes she made herself, familiar to her skin, by dressing elegantly so people stopped on the street to look at her, wondering whether she was a fashion model. When I was young, I loved to see what she would be wearing, what new original she had cut and stitched overnight. But by the time I was an adolescent, I wanted her to dress like everybody else's mother, in sensible clothes, skirts and sweaters, penny loafers and knee socks, and not as if she had fallen out of the pages of the French *Vogue* pattern book she kept on her bedside table. I wanted her to buy my clothes off the rack too.

But not that summer in Warm Springs. Just to see her coming toward me took my breath away.

She sat down and pulled up the chair next to my bed.

"Dr. Iler says you are doing wonderfully," she said. "You look much better this morning."

"How can you tell?" I asked.

"The color in your cheeks," she said.

My mother determined everything by the color in my cheeks, which were inclined to yellow.

"I hear Lindsey is sick."

"She is sick." Her voice was tentative.

"How sick?" I asked, determined not to let on that it made a difference whether Lindsey was ill or just feigning illness, as I believed she was doing so she could go home.

"I think the heat has gotten the best of her."

"Then maybe she should leave," I said.

There was a long pause, and then my mother talked about the operation and its success and what Dr. Iler had to say about the future — two months in a cast, then a peek at how the surgery had worked, and if it had been as successful as the doctor thought, I'd begin physical therapy, walking between the bars, soaking in hot paraffin, swimming in the baths. And then a second transplant, once they saw how the therapy had worked. And maybe — just a possibility — the transplant would have worked so well, a second operation would not be necessary. This I remember.

My mother was direct, and it wasn't like her to suggest the possibility that I might leave Warm Springs early if she had not been under pressure to compensate for something I didn't know.

"Maybe Lindsey could take a train back to Columbus and a taxi to Urbana," I said.

"I don't think she'll be willing to do that."

I was twelve that summer, my mother thirty-nine, and Lindsey fifty-four. I *know* fifty-four. It isn't old and wasn't then. Her heart was fine, although she always talked about it. Jeffie and I used to say that Lindsey Greene didn't have one, that there was just a hole in her chest for a heart. She would live to be one hundred and three, outliving my mother by more than twenty years.

"I'm taking Lindsey home," my mother said, her voice neither exploratory nor apologetic. "It's very hot, hot for her at least, and she has a heart condition, or perhaps she has something with her heart, but under the circumstances and because you're such a grown-up . . ." She could go on and on, especially when she was nervous. "I think we're leaving this afternoon for Ohio." And then she added, to be sure I understood, "We are leaving this afternoon."

"That's fine," I said, without a missed beat, quick to rebound, to construct a mechanism concealing disappointment even from myself. "Soon I'll be back in my wheelchair and can go anyplace I wish."

"Of course you will," she said, relieved.

Apparently Dr. Iler had reassured her that I was well enough for her to leave, that Miss Riley would pay special attention to me.

"If you're even the least bit sick or upset or unhappy," she told me, "I'll be back in a flash."

"On an airplane?" I asked, and she laughed and so did I, since we both knew that my mother didn't fly in airplanes.

My mother stayed most of that second day with me, a day of practical advice for getting through the next couple of months, when she'd be back to visit. She brought me sanitary napkins and some candy and a new nightgown and said she would send books from Washington to read.

"Since you don't want to have tutoring," she said. "What books would you like me to send?"

"Big-family books, like *Five Little Peppers and How They Grew* and *Little Women* and *Cheaper by the Dozen* — books about a child in a huge family with a lot happening all the time."

"I'll send you my collection of Little Colonel stories about Virginia Lloyd," she said. These were my mother's favorite childhood books, a Victorian series about a young girl, like Nancy Drew but domestic and without the element of mystery.

"Don't worry about sending the Little Colonel," I said. "Nothing happens, and her family is too small."

I didn't watch her leave.

"Is your mom going for good?" Sandy Newcombe asked.

"We have a family emergency," I said. "And I'm fine by myself."

For years, I didn't remember that she had left precipitously the second day after my surgery. I recalled only having vague misgivings about my second stay in Warm Springs and why it had ended the way it did.

Years later, when I was in my thirties, my mother, in her sixties, was dying, although we didn't know it at the time. It was June of the summer that she died, in August, and she brought up the summer of 1951.

It was evening, and we were sitting on the screened porch of her house, my children were sleeping, and we were talking with the same ease we had had all my life.

She had something to tell me.

Now I think that she sensed she might be dying and wanted to put things in some kind of order, although I had no particular sense of disorder. She had taught me never to go to bed angry. I believe she lived by that as well as a person could. She was a child in her need for emotional immediacy.

After she died, my brother and I found a spiral notebook of her life. She seemed not to have kept it up for a long time. Its literal language and nonreflective tone, its careful linear chronicle of events, made it important to me only for the facts it included. Among these was a record of her leaving Warm Springs with Lindsey two days after I had surgery. "Morning of third day after Susan's surgery. Left to take Lindsey back to Urbana." She didn't say why she'd left, only that she had.

When my mother died in 1981, her will left everything to Jeffrey and me. Lindsey, then in her mid-eighties, got in her car and drove from Urbana to Washington to meet Jeff and me for lunch.

"She left me nothing," Lindsey said, "not even an ashtray."

We had no reason to speak to her again after that, and didn't. But one winter afternoon when I had gone to Urbana with Jeffrey for the funeral of our aunt Janet — Lindsey's niece, my mother's cousin by marriage — Lindsey drove up to Oakdale Cemetery in her white Cadillac, rolled down the window, and looked at me with a peculiar expression, more like curiosity than anything else.

"Betty?" she asked, calling me by my mother's name, and I believe she thought I was my mother. "I didn't think I'd see you here."

"Well, here I am," I said.

That night on the screened porch, my mother apologized for leaving me alone when I was barely out of surgery.

"I was fine," I said.

"You were not fine," she said.

She wanted me to acknowledge that she had left me there. She wanted me to accept her apology, and I did, although I had only a shimmer of memory about her departure, until much later, when those June days came back of a piece.

I was in bed for almost a week after my mother left, not unusual with surgery at that time. Though the recovery seemed to go on forever, I had a plan in mind.

It was warm and sultry that summer, a sleepy softness to the air, with light breezes coming through the windows of the ward and across our languid bodies. I spent hours, half propped up by a pillow, lingering over the details of my plan for survival over the next eleven months, more or less without my mother's company.

I would be an entirely different girl. An invention to suit the times, a construct in the long tradition of self-made men and women, and in this case, the goal was goodness.

In my Survival Notebook, I made a list of good works that included visiting one new sick person every day, concentrating on the adult patients and those patients who were actually sick and whom I would be permitted to visit. I'd continue my jobs of mail and bedpans and would write letters to the people I never wrote to, like Grandma Richards and Caroline Slover's mother, who regularly sent me get-well cards. I'd write to Lindsey for the sake of forgiveness — not a virtue I in general pursued — and my teachers at Sidwell Friends, from which I had been more or less expelled. I would get in touch with Miss Forkman and start up tutoring, and I would obey the rules of Warm Springs and respect those in authority.

I had never been a good girl, in the conventional perception of goodness as obedience, and at some level I knew that I needed a self-corrective list, as if I were learning a new language and had to practice my verbs by constant repetition of their conjugation.

"Good girl" was a term widely used in the fifties. An expectation, a ticket of admission, a rule of life in an atmosphere of rules. It usually referred to sexual behavior, but it had a trickle-down effect. At eleven or twelve or even younger, success for a girl was goodness and selection for the cheerleading squad, not a contradictory pairing in those years.

Sometime in 1951, *The Power of Positive Thinking,* by the Protestant minister Norman Vincent Peale, was published. It struck an immediate chord among postwar Americans. We were a great country, victors at war and at home, economically successful, a forceful challenge to the Communists, God- and family-centered, reproducing like rabbits into a promising future, clean and virtuous and good. It was for so many Americans, especially in the provinces, a period in which the Puritan virtues of hard work and strong moral values triumphed, and being different was considered suspect, even un-American. There was a conviction reflected in *The Power of Positive Thinking* that individual will could prevail; it was only a matter of believing in it.

The Catcher in the Rye was published in 1951 as well. Holden Caulfield's story of hypocrisy and alienation captured a generation of young Americans with its new voice of outrage. Ethel and Julius Rosenberg were sentenced to death for transmitting atomic secrets as spies for the Soviet Union. The Communist Party was effectively outlawed in a decision handed down by the Supreme Court, *Dennis v. United States.* And the first postwar nuclear test on American soil occurred at the Nevada Test Site, not far from Las Vegas; the government assured the area's residents that there was no danger. In fact, radioactive fallout contaminated the atmosphere as far as two hundred miles away, causing radiation-connected illnesses, denied by the government for years.

In Jonas Salk's laboratory at the University of Pittsburgh, researchers with funding from the National Foundation for Infantile Paralysis, supported by the March of Dimes and other extraordinary volunteer fund-raising efforts, were, in 1951, close to a field trial of a polio vaccine.

By the time I was dismissed from bed rest after surgery, my bed had been moved three places to the right along the wall, next to Avie Crider on one side and Anna Fitz on the other. Sandy Newcombe and her endless chatter were next to the door.

In those first weeks after my mother left, traveling first to Urbana to drop off Lindsey and then to Columbus, where my father flew to join her so she didn't have to drive home alone, she wrote me two or three letters a day. She had taken up drawing. The pictures she sent were little squiggles at the end of a letter, of a girl in a wheelchair with very large wheels and the girl's hair sticking straight up, giving the impression that she was moving very fast. I loved these pictures. They brought me the whimsical mother I knew, which her literal, newsy letters did not reveal.

And I'd write back full of the happy inventions of daily life at Warm Springs.

I never thought about her leaving with Lindsey. And if I had, I would have placed the blame on Lindsey, not my mother.

I filled every moment of my day from breakfast to lights out with work, leaving little time to think. That was good.

The second stay at Warm Springs had taken on a different tone. Pensive, sometimes melancholy, tentative. I was twelve, somewhere between childhood and something else. Tentative and melancholy were not adjectives I had associated with myself before. Living in my own body had come to feel precarious, as if I were on a balancing bar and had to pay attention.

The list I made in my Survival Notebook looked something like this:

7:00 A.M. Breakfast
7:30 A.M. Bedpans
8:30 A.M. Visit Adult Ward, room 12, with cookies

I got cookies from the candy store and took them, three or four in a paper napkin, as a gift when I went to visit patients, something I had learned from Grandma Richards, who traveled everywhere with cookies in her purse, just in case she met someone she liked.

9:00 A.M. Babies' Ward
10:00 A.M. Tutoring with Miss Forkman (Tuesday and
Thursday)
11:30 A.M. Lunch
12:00–2:00 P.M. Read. Talk to one of the girls in the ward.

I went around the room with a plan to talk to the patients confined to bed, so that by the end of two weeks, every two weeks, I
would have spent time with each of them. Given a choice, I might
have spent all of my time with Avie Crider, but according to my
own rules, I had to spend the same amount of time with Sandy
Newcombe.

2:00 P.M. Mail delivery
4:00 P.M. Bedpans
5:00 P.M. Dinner
6:00 P.M. Joey
7:30 P.M. Bed

Nighttime in the ward was cozy. We giggled and whispered. We
sang together and told outrageous stories of what we might do
when we got out. Often someone would start a story and it would
go around the room from bed to bed, each of us adding to it when
our turn came.

Those nights were as close as I got to a sense of family at Warm
Springs, as close as I have ever felt to belonging to a group.

All that summer and fall of 1951, I kept to my Florence Nightin-
gale routine of good works, waking up every morning relieved to
have my day planned down to the last minute, including the visits
I would make in the various rooms, unaware that the life I was
leading was one of lonely desperation.

Whatever had happened between my mother and me when she
left with Lindsey, I had turned into an escape artist.

There wasn't an excess of sympathy from my mother. No indul-
gences. No special considerations. A handicap was a handicap and
no more.

*   *   *

When I had children, there were always special considerations. Whether I consciously chose to be different from my mother or was unconsciously making up for what I had missed or was simply a mother of my time, an offshoot of the sixties, I was looser with rules, more indulgent in the child-centered, freewheeling household I created, full of noise and cats and dogs and a certain amount of unbridled confusion.

My children, now grown, tell me they will make *their* children go to school every day and on time, unless they have a high fever.

I would have been a different person without my mother's perseverance. I would have been different without Warm Springs.

At the very heart of fiction — and writing fiction is what I have done all my professional life — is character and change. Does the character, in the most simplistic sense, change as a result of what happens to him in the story? We want to think one thing leads to another. We have the need to believe that life experiences matter.

My mother was not unusual among the caretakers of polios, including Eleanor Roosevelt, who pushed their charges to live beyond their limitations.

I look at the pictures of Franklin Roosevelt differently than I did when I started to write this memoir. Before, I saw his strong, smiling face, his powerful torso and shapely hands, the physical force of his presence. And just as he would have wished, I didn't see the wheelchair or the crutches or the tight grip of a man standing next to him, holding him up.

What I see in photographs now is the courage of his laughter, the pain of standing, the ten-pound weight of steel he carried on his legs and how it wore him down. This giant of a man sitting in the company of standing men, no taller than he was and of no more force. What it must have taken to be that man. He wanted the life he had, and he must have loved it, but it came at great cost and with powerful loneliness.

I don't claim this as my story; it is the story of most of the children with whom I lived at Warm Springs. *The Power of Posi-*

tive Thinking was in their blood. They didn't need to read the book.

In the past twenty years, a new condition has been discovered among polios called post-polio syndrome, which seems to have affected about 50 percent of the people who had polio decades earlier. The symptoms are general weakness, a loss of muscle control, and in some cases the return to a wheelchair, even to bed. These symptoms are similar to the original illness, including the pain associated with the onset of the virus. Physicians and scientists have concluded that the previously determined, ambitious, hard-driving polios have perhaps worn out the ancillary muscles, and the body has given up.

I was asked several years ago whether I'd agree to be part of a research study, in a control group of patients who had not yet experienced post-polio syndrome, and I refused. At the time, my reason was simple: I was suggestible, and I felt that I'd end up with post-polio if I joined the group.

In retrospect, and as a result of the reading I have done for this book, I believe I reacted to type. Again and again, it's reported that we polios didn't look back, didn't dwell on the negative, didn't concern ourselves with impossibilities. We were proficient at denial.

I believe there is a physical, instinctive explanation for this. Those of us who had paralytic polio generally were left with traces of muscles and the confidence — another word for hope — that those muscles could be restored. It took hours and days and weeks of concentration on a very small part of the body to work on a trace of muscle. It was tedious, repetitious, and the rewards were small.

The process lends itself to that of a competitive athlete, practicing over and over again the same move, the same stroke, with the same perseverance. Or it lends itself to becoming a writer.

*　　*　　*

I saw Joey Buckley on my first day up from surgery. I was wheeling from one end of the corridor to the other, and Joey was just coming out of the Boys' Ward.

He saw me and waited just outside his ward.

"So you're back," he said.

"You too," I said.

"We ought to do some fun stuff this time, don't you think?" he asked.

"We will," I said, and, hardly able to contain my tears of laughter, "we will, we will, we will."

March of Dimes Day

I WOKE UP ONE Sunday morning with the idea for March of Dimes Day already in my head, as if it were the tail end of a dream. It was early July, after a long and lonely weekend when some of the nearby parents from Georgia, Alabama, North Carolina, and Tennessee had driven over to visit their children, as they sometimes did on weekends, and Joey Buckley had gone home for the week to get over the croup. The hospital had been too quiet, the air so hot and still, even with the fans going, that I wanted to sleep clear through until Monday.

Instead I sat up in bed and made a diagram of Ward 8, a drawing of the beds with the names of the girls, ten of them that July, since some had gone home for good at the end of June and Avie Crider was having a holiday with her parents in St. Paul and Julie Camp had come down with something catching, so she'd been moved to isolation.

By the time the breakfast trays were delivered, my plan for March of Dimes Day was beginning to take shape.

I have always been a starter of things. In retrospect, my drive for new beginnings was born of loneliness more than a desire for leadership. As a child growing up in the years of birthday parties and sleepovers and exclusive clubs of girls, I must have come to the self-protective decision that in case I wasn't going to be invited to the party, then I would have the party myself.

I had written a newspaper that I distributed in the neighborhood, full of maxims and other earnest hints for leading a better life, what I must have assumed was helpful instruction for the families in Cleveland Park. Again, these were the postwar years of high moral purpose, of discomfort with ambiguity, a kind of cheerful smugness. I fell right into line, in spite of my questionable behavior at school, recommending such axioms of good behavior as my personal favorite at the time, from "Outwitted" by Edwin Markham, which I had lifted from a pamphlet and used as the banner of one of my newspapers, the *Cleveland Park Weekly:* "*He drew a circle that shut me out / Heretic, rebel, a thing to flout / But love and I had the wit to win / We drew a circle that took him in.*"

I had also formed a small acting company, consisting of Jeffie and me and General Beauregard, and we performed plays for profit in our living room. I wrote one called *Mercy, Be Kind to the Indians,* playing the part of Mercy myself, with Jeffie as the Indian boy and General Beauregard as the horse. In the summer I had put together a neighborhood circus for the younger children and made a clubhouse under one of the porches on our street, where I served magic lollipops and told stories to the little children in the semidarkness.

My need for the March of Dimes Day had come shortly after the Fourth of July, when I received a letter from Lindsey Greene, my stepgrandmother, who had returned to the cool breezes of Urbana, Ohio, to play bridge at the country club. The letter went something like this (I don't have the letter in hand to support this memory, though her letters were more or less interchangeable):

Dear Susan,

I trust it's cooler there than when I left. I can't imagine anyone living in the kind of heat they have in Georgia. No wonder! ["No wonder" was a phrase dear to her heart, which stood for most anything; in this case I imagine it stood for *No wonder I had to leave Warm Springs.*] I was at the five-and-ten yesterday, where your other grandmother ["other grandmother" was the best she could do in identifying

Grandma Richards, known with great affection in their community as Aunt Bessie] works at the costume jewelry coun-
ter, and she stopped me as I was about to purchase some
nylons and said that your great-uncle Harry or Joe, I can't
remember which, but you don't know him well, had died on
Thursday and was being buried that afternoon. She didn't
mention the cause of his death, but I happen to know he had
a drinking problem . . .

I'm sure that in the second paragraph she said she hoped that I
was doing well and had some friends and not to eat too much
greasy food like they seemed to favor in the South.

I phoned my parents right away. The staff let me call even
though it was the middle of the week and usually I called on
weekends, but I told the receptionist at the front desk that someone had died in my family, and she placed the call for me.

"Who died?" I asked when my mother answered the phone and
my heart was beating hard.

There was a long pause.

"Uncle Joe," my mother said finally. "Grandma Richards's oldest brother, but I didn't think it necessary to tell you, darling.
What could you do about it but worry, and I would have told you
when we saw each other next."

She was right about the worry. I could hardly breathe for thinking about death — not Uncle Joe's death, which wasn't surprising
since he was quite an old man, probably in his eighties. I didn't
know him well but I did know him, and I'd had dinner at his
house every time we visited Urbana. Lately, in the past year, he
had been getting up from the dinner table, pulling open one of
the drawers of the buffet where the napkins were kept, and peeing
in it. This didn't seem to bother anyone, certainly not his wife
or even my mother and father, but Jeff and I giggled into our
napkins, leaning up against our cousins, and almost choked on
our food.

"He has quite a bit of beer before he sits down at the table," my
mother told me. "And he's too old to hold his pee."

"I'm not even going to the funeral, darling," my mother said, as though that would make some difference in the fact of death. "He was very old and it was to be expected."

Death was to be expected. That stuck with me, although I'm quite sure that my mother said that to ease my mind, to take the fear of death out of our conversation, but of course my mind was already on a different path, galloping toward darkness. Here I was in this outpost of crippled children, stuck with others who couldn't get away, couldn't get farther than the hospital candy store on their own in a wheelchair, and what could I do with such a possibility as death menacing the lives of the people I loved, the people on whom my life depended?

Death was kept behind closed doors in the middle-class families of those postwar years, parents who had grown up with their own parents dying at home, slow deaths in which the family participated. Dying was not the secret that it was for my postwar generation of children, accumulating, as death did for us, the kind of terrifying danger of the secret.

I couldn't sleep that night for thinking of Uncle Joe. His face turned into the face of my father, and I wondered, Was he lying in a casket with his face showing, bone white with his mouth and eyes closed? Then I started thinking about my parents: if one of them had to die, which one would I choose, which one could I bear to do without? That night my breath came in short takes, and when I woke up in the morning I was thinking of the March of Dimes.

The actual March of Dimes was initiated by the National Foundation for Infantile Paralysis in 1938 as part of its fund-raising campaign and was given its name by the beloved comedian Eddie Cantor. The foundation was a private charity started by Roosevelt and Basil O'Connor, administered by O'Connor with the goal of raising funds for the care and cure of poliomyelitis.

Eddie Cantor represented the perfect husband and father in the idealized American family of the time, publicly devoted to his wife and five daughters. Through his radio show he created a bond with families all over the country. He loved Roosevelt, and in the foundation's courting of Hollywood, he became the celebrity to take a central role in its mission to eliminate polio. Cantor launched the March of Dimes on his show, entreating the American people to send their dimes directly to the president in the White House. He alerted the White House mailroom that the volume of mail might increase. In fact, it went from 30,000 letters on the day the campaign started to 150,000 by the third day. The letters had to be redirected from the White House in order for the initiative to function, but the campaign had begun, uniting the nation in collecting dimes for the protection of the health of its children. The campaign culminated eight years later — nine months after FDR's death — with the minting of the Roosevelt dime, in honor of the president's sixty-fourth birthday, January 30, 1946.

This was the same year that the March of Dimes introduced the first polio poster child.

Anyone growing up in those years knew the poster children. Their photographs were seen everywhere in the country and promised a bright future for those ravaged bodies with happy faces.

In the persuasive spirit of advertising and marketing, the chosen poster child was always well groomed, attractive, engaging, and supremely cheerful. Such an encouraging image would attract the attention of the American public and compel people to make a contribution to this child's future, to the future of all children with polio.

In 1946 polio was not nearly as pervasive as the dread of polio. It was true, however, that by the late forties epidemics had increased at a steady and disturbing rate. Under the leadership of Basil O'Connor, the foundation was determined to find a cure.

The first poster child was Donald Anderson, a boy from a working-class family in a small town in Oregon. He had been photographed by a volunteer as a three-year-old, looking out of his crib with a "wistful look" and "enormous eyes." His appeal as

an innocent child destroyed by infantile paralysis must have captured people's hearts. One photograph on the 1946 March of
Dimes poster showed Donald in his crib, braced and bandaged. In
another, taken when he was six, he seems to have recovered and is
striding, full of determination and high spirits, his arms swinging,
his legs moving without support. It was not a factual representa-
tion of the daily life of Donald Anderson, who did not have an
easy time of polio and was certainly not recovered. But the photograph assured the American people that their accumulating dimes
were making a significant difference.

"Your dimes did this for me!" reads the banner across the top of
the poster.

Happy-faced crippled children were used for this campaign,
and surely many of us who had had polio thought about our own
chances at momentary fame.

After breakfast in the Girls' Ward, I made a speech. In the heat of
early July in Georgia, we often stayed in bed, those of us with the
choice of getting into wheelchairs, until the breakfast trays were
taken.

This was my plan for March of Dimes Day. We would all com-
pete to be the poster child for 1952, the year ahead. I imagined a
committee of people from the National Foundation for Infantile
Paralysis coming to the Girls' Ward. Basil O'Connor would be
among them. We all knew his name, believing, as was more or less
true, that we owed our medical care to him. This group of digni-
taries would photograph each of us, and we'd tell them our personal polio story, and then one among us would be chosen as the
poster child.

In this game of the March of Dimes, we would not be ourselves.
We would create a persona, invent a dramatic story such as the
one contrived by the foundation for Donald Anderson, recreate
ourselves as an advertisement for polio recovery in order to earn
us consideration as the polio poster child.

That was the game. Only we, the girls of Ward 8, would know what was going on. Not the nurses, not the patients, not doctors or orderlies. One morning, maybe in mid-July, we'd begin as someone other than who we were, with a story to tell worthy of engaging the sympathies of the American people.

If you entered the Girls' Ward that early July and turned right, you'd see that the beds lined up along the near wall were assigned to me, Polly, Jennifer, Marianna, and Sandy Newcombe, with an empty bed left for Avie. On the other side of the room were Amy's bed, Elaine's, Julie's bed, empty while she was in isolation, Bootsie's, Janet's, and Francy's.

"I don't understand this game." Polly was a small blond girl, crippled below the waist, pretty, stoic, and cheerless. "I don't want to play."

"It's not exactly a game," Marianna said. "You don't *play* it."

I didn't know Marianna well. I had been back at Warm Springs for only three weeks, two of them following surgery, after Lindsey Greene took my mother away, but so far I liked Marianna and Avie the best.

It is curious to me now, as a person who holds tight to friendship, that all of these associations except for mine with Caroline have slipped away except in memory. And even Caroline has not been in my life for years. I don't know what to make of that except to conclude we were all young, homesick, self-centered, probably afraid and too proud to show it, determined to get better, biding time until we could return to our lives. Perhaps we didn't even want to hold on to those years. Were it not for the novel I wrote in the wake of leaving, those two years in Warm Springs might have been simply among the inadvertent losses I have had in my life. But I remember the ward and the feeling of friendship in it, the smell and sound of it, and the faces of those girls. It was, I think, a place to be *in the moment*. And after the moment it was time to be someplace else.

"So show us how it will go," Janet said from her bed, to which she had been confined for months in a body cast with slow-healing back surgery.

"Like this," I began. "The judges, whoever they're going to be, come in the room and I say, *I am Susan Richards, and I got polio when I was a baby in Toledo, Ohio, and was paralyzed from the neck down.*" I exaggerated an enormous smile. I was not a smiley girl, but I arranged one for the occasion. "*And then my parents got a divorce and I went to live in an orphanage, where the nuns were extremely cruel to girls who weren't blond and weren't perfect,*" I went on cheerfully. "*And finally I was adopted by a very kind man who was a clown in the Ringling Brothers circus, and he started teaching me to walk in braces even though I was in terrible pain, and then he heard about Warm Springs. So here I am, and when I leave I'm going to be fine.*"

"Did your parents really get a divorce?" Bootsie asked.

"They didn't," I said. "My parents will never get a divorce."

"Is any of that story true?" Bootsie asked.

"I was born in Toledo and was paralyzed. That part is true."

"So you're not an orphan," Polly said.

"I'm not," I said. "Pretty much the rest I made up."

"We're all going to make up who we are then, right?" Polly asked. "That's kind of like lying."

"No it's not," Marianna said. "It's like telling a story, which is different from lying."

"So that's all we do," Polly said. "Make up a story?"

"We have to smile," I said. "We have to act like we're getting better and better and polio is nothing to us, hardly a bother at all."

And so our plans were made that morning, and we wrote down the rules:

1. We would tell no one who we were until March of Dimes Day.

2. March of Dimes Day would start the morning of July 15.

3. Father James would be told of our plan. He'd be the only one told, and he'd bring the nurses and orderlies in and they would choose the 1952 poster child.

4. We wouldn't say one word to the doctors and nurses and orderlies about our plan.

"Who will judge us?" Marianna asked.
"We'll judge ourselves," Elaine said. "We'll do a secret ballot and
vote and Miss Riley will count the votes."

Ward 8 came alive. For days, whenever the nurses weren't in the
room, we practiced our stories back and forth. Or we shut the
door and all played our pretend roles as if we were the subjects of
our own invention. And when the nurses did come or the orderlies arrived to take one of us to the plaster room or the brace shop
or to physical therapy, we stopped pretending and giggled, bury-
ing our faces in our pillows or picking up a book and hiding behind the pages. At night we sang our favorite songs together:
"When the Saints Go Marching In" or "Put another muscle in /
Where the quadriceps have been / 'Cause we know we'll never win
/ With traces, traces, traces." Or songs we heard from our mothers
when we were very small, like, "Oh little playmate / Please come
and play with me / And bring your dollies three / Climb up
my apple tree / Slide down my rain barrel / Look down my cellar
door / And we'll be jolly friends / Forevermore." Or "I want
to dance with the dolly with a hole in her stocking / While her
knees keep a knocking and her toes keep a rocking / Want to
dance with the dolly with a hole in her stocking / Want to dance
by the light of the moon." The same songs night after night until
Miss Riley came in to say "Lights out," and then we whispered
into the darkness.

One night, she stood in the doorway after the lights were out.
"What is going on with you girls?"
"Nothing," we said in unison.
"Nothing?"
"Nothing at all," I said. "We're just becoming good friends."
"I think you're becoming too good friends," Miss Riley said,

and pulled the door almost closed so the light in the hall didn't keep us awake.

But we stayed awake. We were always getting ready for March of Dimes Day.

The morning of July 15 was hot even before the sun rose. A new girl had been admitted the night before, in the last bed against the far wall. Her name was Angela, and that night while we giggled in our beds, she was crying softly, her back to us. We knew from one of the orderlies that she would be having surgery in two days, which meant that on March of Dimes Day she wouldn't be in the ward but downstairs having a physical and other tests. We were relieved to have her gone, and it was lucky, we all said, that Angela had not been admitted the day before, or else on March of Dimes Day she would have been in the first bed, post-operative and probably screaming out in pain, as happened to all of us when we came out of anesthesia.

But Avie was back and so was Julie, so the beds were almost full.

"I suppose you know that one of us is going to be the poster child this year," Polly said to Miss Anna when she came in with the breakfast trays. Miss Anna was new that summer, just out of nursing school, and what I remember about her is her crackling laughter and big freckled hands.

"One of you girls is going to be the poster child?" she asked.

We nodded.

"One of us," I said. "We're all under consideration."

"How come I didn't know about this?" Miss Anna asked.

"No reason you should know. We find out today."

"I suppose you know what the poster child is, don't you?" Janet asked.

"Who doesn't?" Miss Anna said. "The posters are hanging all over hell and gone. Some little blond angel is the poster child this year."

She stood at the door and looked around the room. "Something crazy's going on here," she said.

We all had big smiles on our faces as if we'd been practicing happiness, which we had been, sitting up straight in bed if we could sit up, or our heads raised out of body casts like turtles.

"Well, they were looking for a girl again this year," I said, "and they decided to look in the Girls' Ward at Warm Springs."

"Well I'll be darned," Miss Anna said.

One of the orderlies, called Jimbo, came to take Angela downstairs to have her physical, and Miss Anna stopped him.

"Do you know those polio poster kids, Jimbo?" she asked. "All smiles and skinny with braces heavy as dump trucks on their legs and big corsets so they can sit up happy as clams?"

"I know those pictures," Jimbo said. "We've got one next door to my place at the drugstore."

"Well, one of these girls might be the poster child next year."

"No kidding?" Jimbo said, lifting Angela into a wheelchair. "How do you get to be a poster child?"

"You have to have a terrible story," I said. "And smile a lot."

"So give me a terrible story," he said, directing his remark to Bootsie, who was sitting in bed, her legs dangling over the side, her eyes dancing.

"I got polio in the swimming pool at the playground down the street when I was seven, and some kids got it and died, and I almost died but I didn't. And then my parents were so fed up because they had to carry me everyplace that they gave me to my grandmother, and now I'm here because there were enough dimes collected to get me here and get me better and now I'm almost well."

"I guess you are," Miss Anna said.

"Is that a true story?" Jimbo asked.

"Every bit of it is true," Bootsie said.

"I thought I met your mother."

"Bootsie's mother came but she didn't stay like my mother

didn't stay, so it's been Bootsie here for almost a year," Janet said. "And not even one person has come to visit her, so she's getting well all by herself."

"I see that," Jimbo said.

Janet had the worst story, and part of it was actually true, like the story of Rosie in the Babies' Ward.

"I got polio when I was five in Oregon and my little sister died of it and my big brother almost died and is still in an iron lung and I was in an iron lung for six months and now look at me."

"You don't look all that good to me," Jimbo said. "Not 'til you cut loose of that plaster."

"I'm going to be fine," Janet said. "I'm going to walk out of here without braces or crutches and I'm giving away my wheelchair to Bootsie."

"What about you, Polly?"

"I got polio when I was three, and we were on the only vacation my parents had ever taken. I was the youngest child of five children, and now they'll never be able to take another vacation because I can't walk and it's a lot of trouble for my parents. And that's all."

"You're less trouble than anyone I know, Polly," Jimbo said.

"Except to my mother. She takes care of me all the time."

"You didn't make anything up," I whispered to Polly.

"I can't make things up," Polly said. "I would've done it but I just don't know how."

Jimbo pushed Angela out the door, passing Miss Riley, who came in with laxatives and other meds.

"What's this I hear about a poster child in this ward?" Miss Riley asked. "This is not exactly a poster child ward."

"What does that mean?" I asked.

"It means what it says," Miss Riley went on. "And how come I never heard about this before?"

"We didn't have a chance to tell you."

"Well, who told you?" she asked.

I was the best liar in the group, the most practiced liar.

"My father knows Basil O'Connor," I said, "and he recommended to Mr. O'Connor that he look for the poster child in our ward."

"I think Mr. O'Connor should be thinking about raising the salaries of the nursing staff instead of looking for poster children," Miss Riley said.

"He's maybe doing that too," I added for good luck.

Father James, who had been alerted to the contest, arrived at lunchtime and listened to Sandy Newcombe's story about catching polio in Georgia at her aunt's house and not being able to get out of bed when she woke up in the morning.

"You were all invited to try out for poster child?" Father James asked.

"We were," Bootsie said. "They thought it would be a good idea to find a girl at Warm Springs to put on a happy, get-better-and-better-every-day face, and that's who we are, all of us."

"Not every day," Father James said, sitting down beside Polly, running his fingers through her hair. "And Polly, it's very nice to see you so cheerful."

"I would like to win," Polly said quietly.

"Wouldn't everybody like to win?" he asked.

"I'd like to win the most," Polly said. "It would make my mother very happy."

I remember that in particular — remember how many times I wanted to do something to balance the sadness I had brought my own mother. But I never would have said it out loud, never would have wanted anyone to know how much I counted on my mother's happiness for my own. Had it taken courage, I wondered, for Polly to tell the real truth about herself, or was she by nature incapable of invention?

"What about you?" Father James asked, leaning over my bed.

I shrugged.

"I won't win," I said. I didn't add, "I'm not sick enough," but that is what I was thinking.

"I heard you were sent to an orphanage when you were small, yes?" He was smiling.

"That's right," I said, "but not for long."

We voted after dinner, and I was chosen to count the votes. I tore off pieces of notebook paper and passed them around the room, then collected the votes while everybody waited, watching.

"I bet it's Janet," Sandy Newcombe said.

"It won't be me," Janet said. "I didn't vote for myself."

"Me neither," Sandy said.

"Me neither," Bootsie said.

I opened the votes one by one, putting them face-up on my bed.

Polly. Polly. Polly. Polly. Polly . . .

Everyone had voted for Polly.

That night I couldn't go to sleep. The breathing of the girls, no different from any other night, was thunder in my ears.

"It was fun, Suzie," Bootsie called across the room.

"It really was fun," Janet said.

"I liked best that we all did this together," Avie said.

"That it was our own private secret," Polly said.

And everybody clapped. They clapped so loudly that Miss Riley came in and told us to hush or we'd wake the babies on the floor below. Then she walked over to my bed.

"I'm leaving a note from Joey Buckley on your bedside table," she said.

"Can I turn on the light and read it?" I asked, my heart leaping.

"I've read it already. All it says is he wants to meet you tomorrow morning and go to the candy store. He has a new wheelchair."

"Tell him yes," I said. "Tell him I'll meet him first thing in the morning after breakfast."

I listened to the steady tread of her oxfords across the linoleum floor.

"Silence from now on, girls," she said, closing our door. "Did you hear me?"

"Yes," we said in unison.

I heard her voice in the distance, speaking to one of the night nurses, and then the hall was silent.

"Thank you for clapping, everybody," I said after Miss Riley had gone.

A Changing Friendship

*F*ATHER JAMES CALLED me into the office on the ground floor of Second Medical and said he had something he wanted to talk to me about.

I wheeled in and pulled up next to his desk.

Except for March of Dimes Day in Ward 8, I hadn't seen much of him since June. He'd been especially busy, having taken on a parish in the next village, and he was spending only two days a week at Warm Springs. We had dropped catechism classes until early spring, which worked for me since I was busy myself, with my self-betterment program and other things. Including Joey Buckley.

"How is everything going?" he asked.

"Really good," I said. "I'm very happy here."

I think I *was* happy that fall. The nurses, especially Miss Riley, seemed glad to have me back. Dr. Iler said he had heard good things about me. I had been well known during my first stay, but the staff were wary of me, expecting a disturbance when I was around. I was beginning to find a new place for myself. I still didn't understand what had gone wrong with Magnolia, why I had been in so much trouble for that friendship. I continued to play with her the two days she was at Warm Springs, but we played under the table, where she'd been told to stay, and I didn't take her on wheelchair rides.

I felt subdued, as if some of my former self had dropped out and I was left with the shell of the girl I'd been. But it wasn't bad.

The rise in my approval rating filled me with a kind of mirth. I couldn't believe how easy it was to be good.

That was the first thing Father James said.

"I've heard good things," he said. "Great things. When you were here last year, you were always in trouble here and there, dragging Magnolia into the Children's Ward, invading the Boys' Ward. You seem to have settled down."

He looked different, maybe older. He did have more gray in the semicircle of hair around the crown of his head and wrinkles on the sides of his eyes. But something else had changed. I wasn't sure what was unfamiliar, only that I could see it.

I didn't want to appear settled down, exactly. Not with Father James. I'd seen enough movies to prefer a walk-on-the-wild-side girl. I took the films that we saw every Saturday to heart. Especially the love scenes.

"Do you know about sex?" I asked Joey Buckley once.

"I don't *talk* about it, if that's what you mean."

"That's not what I mean," I said. "I mean do you know stuff."

But Joey was finished with the conversation before it even got started. He reached into his pocket, took out a cigarette, and stuck it behind my ear.

"Don't smoke it," he said. "We're not allowed."

Father James got up from the desk, walked over, and pulled a chair up next to mine, crossing his legs at the knee.

"Miss Riley said you're winning the good citizenship award."

"Is there a good citizenship award?"

"If there were one, you'd win it, is what she said."

It was, I thought later, what I had wanted. An award for citizenship. To be admired if not loved. Loved was something else, only possible with the very few people who knew me inside out and who, knowing the inside, forgave the outside. That would be my mother and my father and maybe Jeffrey. Not a large group. But I was hoping, before I left Warm Springs, to include in it Father James and Joey Buckley.

"What I want to talk to you about is Joey Buckley," he said.

There was a mark on his face I hadn't noticed before, a darkness on one cheek that ran the length of it, as if he had been accidentally burned, and then I wondered whether I had seen it before and thought it was dirt.

"We're getting to be good friends."

I could feel a cautionary tale in progress.

"Good friends, I know. And that's great. But I was thinking . . . actually Miss Riley brought it up. I was thinking you ought to know something about the relationship between girls and boys at your age."

"I don't want to know anything like that from you," I said.

I started for the door, and he grabbed the arm of my wheelchair.

"I have one more thing to talk to you about."

I don't know whether I was embarrassed or caught in my secret fantasies or simply too young, too immature, to deal with an unedited conversation about sex.

"Do you still want to become a Catholic?"

"I don't know," I said. I would have said yes if I'd been given a second chance. I did want to be a Catholic, but maybe less than I had before. I still loved the mystery and excitement of the rituals, but I no longer *needed* Catholicism in the way I had when religion had to do with a need for safety and an erotic attraction to Father James, and the two seemed one when I wanted the body and the blood.

Now I had a private life. Sometime that fall, when I was wheeling from one place to the next with a purpose, always with a purpose, bedpans or mail or gestures of friendship, I recognized in the empty vat of my chest something like substance, as if I were in the process of becoming someone familiar, my own best friend traveling always at my side.

"For the moment, I'm putting catechism on the back burner while I get used to this new schedule of having a parish," Father James said. "There are real things we need to talk about. I was thinking about that yesterday."

"What do you mean, real?"

"Day-to-day things to address. For instance, Joey Buckley."

Joey and I had been spending a lot of time together when I wasn't working and he wasn't in physical therapy. Sometimes he came with me to the rooms in Second Medical, sometimes we went to the candy store or wandered along the paths, in and out of buildings, exploring and reexploring the same territory. When I left the Girls' Ward in the morning, I'd bring along things to read to Joey: a letter from my mother or Harold Ickes, something I'd torn out of a movie magazine, a note from my father, which might end with "Senator McCarthy's still at it — and his drinking's worse."

My father took me seriously. We used to joke that he would have preferred that babies be incubated until they were eighteen and fully conversational, but he also talked to me as if I were eighteen. I grew up believing I would never marry, and so I had to have a profession. My father told me maybe once, maybe only by implication, that I *must* have a profession. It made an impression. In my head, what he said to me concluded ". . . because you'll never marry and you'll have to take care of yourself."

He may have said that, but then again, I was always inclined to fill in the blanks. And to be overly sensitive to innuendo. He was a leg man, like many of the Betty Grable generation, and although he was respectful of women, particularly my mother, he did communicate to me a concern that my legs were not up to the competition for men looking to marry.

"Watch your back" was my father's message to me. It was meant to be protective. He was, in general, suspicious of people.

I grew up believing, however, that I might marry, and of course

I'd have a profession. Nevertheless, the label of "old maid" was always lurking in the shadows.

My mother was unwavering in her certainty about my future.

These perceptions left an imprint; I began to scan the territory for possible husbands at a young age, predicting it might take a long time to find one. Joey was an early candidate.

Father James leaned back in his chair and folded his arms across his chest.

"Miss Riley tells me you and Joey are often together, and because I know you very well and because we're friends, I'm going to tell you something confidential about Joey. Can you keep a secret?"

I loved secrets. Growing up in a family with secrets hidden behind every piece of standing furniture, under every rug, I was obsessed with secrets, and so my response came as something of a surprise to me:

"What if I don't want to know?"

Joey was mine.

He had become someone particular to me since the first year we had lived at Warm Springs. Not just a boy, a cute boy with floppy black hair and a boyishness about him that was exciting. But more particular.

He was Joey Buckley. Sometimes when we had pulled ourselves out of our wheelchairs and were sitting on the grass behind the candy store like regular kids, when he was telling me about his house in Alabama and his grandma and the way his father, gruff as he was, got broken up over Joey's illness, I turned liquid. It was as if the substantial insides to which I was accustomed had melted, running warm like blood in my veins, and I simply loved Joey Buckley with all my heart.

Father James told me anyway, in spite of my reservations. He said that Joey's grandma had died in May and that his father had a drinking problem and that Joey had returned to Warm Springs for a series of surgeries that might make the difference between walking and not walking for the rest of his life.

"He thinks he will walk again," Father James said. "That is the problem."

"He might walk, right? Isn't that why he's having all this surgery?"

"It's possible, but not likely, not likely at all, but the doctors think it's worth a try. And Miss Riley tells me you're such a cheerleader with him."

"I am," I said. "That's what I am. A cheerleader with everyone."

"Well, the nursing staff is trying to be realistic with him so he won't be too disappointed."

"What do you want me to say to him?"

I had been optimistic. Of course I'd been optimistic. What else did Joey have to get by on day after day except the hope that maybe there was a small chance he'd get to play football for Alabama? There was, I thought, at least a chance.

"Just don't make a big deal of it," Father James said.

I hadn't made a big deal. I'd listened to Joey talk. I knew what he was hoping for when he left Warm Springs, and I hadn't wanted to disappoint him. And why would I, the daughter of a mother who believed everything was possible under certain conditions, only the conditions were up to you to create.

Besides, what did I know about Joey's future? He could recite every single play in an Alabama victory as reported in the local newspaper, and just his obsession with football won me over.

"Let's say he thinks he will be a football player," Father James said, "and is so sure of it that when the cast comes off and he finds out otherwise, he'll be disappointed. Too disappointed." He got up to open the window over the back lawn, and a breeze crossed the desk, taking his papers with it.

"Do you want me to say he won't be playing football?"

"No."

"Do you want me to say I can't talk with him about football anymore?"

"I don't want you to say that either," Father James said. "But I don't want Joey to believe too much. You understand what I'm saying?"

"I understand," I said, "but I think you're wrong."

Father James had turned his chair to the side, his feet resting on an upturned wastebasket draped with his cassock.

I expected that he might ask me to leave but he did not, and I sat across from him, abstracted, a thought forming in my mind. Before I had a chance to think what it was I was really saying, I blurted out what had been simmering in my mind about Father James for almost a year.

"What really happened to your wife?"

He could have ignored me. I was a twelve-year-old girl with very little understanding of the adult world. I had a sense of grief but no genuine experience with the arc of it in a person's life. I wasn't the right audience for a confession.

Father James leaned back in his chair, his palms together under his chin, his eyes fixed on the expanse of lawn behind the office.

"She died," he said. "Her name was Aleilia, and she died of meningitis the year we married. She was nineteen."

"That's awful," I said, at a loss for what else to say, embarrassed by my invasion of his privacy. "I had meningitis too."

"I've read your records," he said.

"What do they say?" I asked with a sudden sinking feeling that my overall behavior had been marked down permanently.

"I read your medical record. It's the only record on file, if that's what you're asking. Only your diseases. Nothing about your character."

He looked young and surprisingly anxious or uncomfortable, as if he didn't know what to do with his hands, so he laced the fingers in and out, pushed back and forth on his chair, his lips tight, his eyes unfocused.

Something familiar, like an agreeable smell I couldn't identify, had surfaced between us, and it was comforting to be with him in this room, as if we had known each other always.

When I leaf through the events of my childhood, certain moments stop me on the page. That afternoon with Father James was the first time someone had trusted me with a confidence. Astonished and humbled by his trust is what I felt.

"Later," he began, changing the subject. "Maybe even this month, we'll get back to catechism. Doesn't that seem right?" he asked.

"It does seem right," I said, and wheeled out of the room before I said too much or asked him another inappropriate question and ruined our friendship.

I don't know why Father James left to go back to Ireland, only that he did. It was in the late spring after I had left, that much I know. One day he was there and the next he was gone, Caroline Slover wrote me. I didn't have an address for him, and though he might have gotten mine from the medical files and written me, he never did.

Joey was getting ready for reconstructive surgery, scheduled for late March, and I was helping him. Or so I thought. I don't know what he thought, since he never complained and wasn't a great talker.

He was supposed to gain weight, so I brought him Clark bars from the candy store and extra ice cream on the days I passed out trays. I read him stories from the books my mother sent me, and although I don't think he was much interested in literature, he loved to lie on the grass, his legs propped up on the seat of his wheelchair, and listen. I told him about my trick with pain, moving it from one place to another, and we'd lie side by side on the grass, practicing.

We went everywhere we were allowed to go together, as far away — about a mile — as the Little White House, where Roosevelt had lived and died.

"Do you think about President Roosevelt?" I asked him once.

"I never knew him," he said. "My father didn't like him, and he doesn't have a good reputation in our house, so I don't ever think about him."

"I think about him because he was the president of the United States, and he was a polio and wheeled around this place just like us."

"That's why you and me are different," Joey said.

Once his father came from Alabama and took us to the local inn for Sunday lunch, and Joey told his father I was his girlfriend.

"You're too young for a girlfriend, Joey," Mr. Buckley said.

"You're right, I am, Dad," Joey agreed, and we all laughed. I didn't understand the laughter, whether it was a joke or whether in fact they thought I wasn't anything to Joey but a helper.

I sometimes took off his high-top oxfords and rubbed his flimsy chicken feet, which ached from hours trapped in the stiff leather shoes.

We were inseparable. Somehow the nurses had given up worrying over my trips to the Boys' Ward, and I assumed it was because I'd turned into this model child.

I told Joey everything about myself, more than I had told anyone except my mother, and he talked about football and the farm where he lived and the John Deere tractor his father bought secondhand and let him ride on the hood.

Once he started to talk about his mother and then he stopped, saying he didn't want to talk about her dead.

"Talk about her alive, then," I said.

But he couldn't.

One Saturday, Joey and I were heading to the movies together in the middle of the line with other wheelchairs — I was in the front of the line of the Girls' Ward and he was in the back of the line of the Boys' Ward — and we followed the others stringing through the narrow paved paths. There was a long, steep dip of cement walk from the level ground of the first floor of the hospital to the movie theater room on the basement level. We had to drive our wheelchairs very slowly down the hill.

"It'd be fun to race down here, don't you think?" I asked him.

"Pretty fun," he said.

"We'd have to keep control of the wheels, and I'd probably be scared."

"I wouldn't be scared," he said.

"Then maybe when you get out of surgery we'll try the hill," I said. "If you want."

In late March my cast was taken off. The doctors were waiting to see whether I'd need to have another transplant, moving a muscle to my right calf. In the meantime I was in physical therapy, exercising my new calf muscle, walking between the parallel bars. "Face forward and walk in a straight line," the therapists would say as I dragged myself from one end of the bars to the other. I'd reduce the considerable swelling and loosen the muscles by soaking my leg in hot paraffin or lying on an exercise table in the spring pool. Physical therapy was slow and made me restless and bad-tempered. More times than not, I was in worse shape after therapy than I had been before it.

I stopped my daily letters home, the way I had written every night before lights out, and my mother began to call several times a week instead of only on Sunday afternoons.

"What is going on?" she asked. "You're not yourself."

"I'm exactly myself," I said.

My father asked if I would like for them to pay a visit — I had seen them only twice since the fall — and I told him no, I would not like for them to pay a visit at all. Before long, I said, I'd be home for good.

Miss Riley came to the ward one night, pulled up a chair, leaned her starchy white uniform on the bed, and asked me whether something was the matter.

"My mother called you, didn't she," I said. "That's why you're here, I'm sure. You can tell her nothing is the matter with me."

And then one afternoon, lying on the grass with Joey two days before his surgery, reading comic books behind the candy store, I felt a stirring of something I'd felt before but never with such insistence. I rolled over on my back. The air was cool, even for late March in Georgia. Overhead, a small plane not far up in the sky, close enough for us to see the fuzzy line of the propellers, crossed just above where we were lying.

"Joey?" I felt an inexplicable intensity, as if nothing that I knew in life so far was sufficient to describe it, as if I were in some kind of immediate danger or wanted danger to step forward and announce itself.

He looked up from his Superman comic.

"I hope we get to grow up before we die," I said.

"Yeah," he said. "Me too. But that's not what I'm thinking about."

For two weeks after Joey's surgery, I went about my usual workday but wasn't allowed to see him until he was well enough to get into his wheelchair and go outside. We had made a plan for then, and I was patient, at least as patient as a girl of my temperament had a right to expect.

His surgery had gone well, according to Miss Riley when I asked her how he was. He'd be up in a couple of weeks, as expected. His father had come and was staying on for another few days.

I got to see him the day before he was allowed to get out of bed.

I was delivering the mail. When I went through the door of the Boys' Ward, Joey, in an Alabama cap, was sitting up in the first bed, the bottom raised, both legs in long casts. He was eating lunch.

"I get out tomorrow," he said.

"Miss Riley told me."

"It looks good, Dr. Iler said. It looks like maybe not football, because it's a contact sport, but it could be baseball."

"That's really great," I said. "Kind of amazing."

"Yup," he agreed. "Really great."

"We should do something special tomorrow to celebrate."

"Something fun. Something different than lying here in bed all day."

"What do you think about racing the hill?"

"Down the big hill?"

"That's what I was thinking."

"Maybe," Joey said, stretching his arms over his head. "Maybe that's exactly what we should do."

IV

....

Leaving Home

Face Forward and
Walk in a Straight Line

I HAD BEGUN to imagine the day of my departure from Warm Springs. It would be late May, toward the end of school in Washington, so I'd have a chance to visit my friends at Sidwell, to let them know that I'd gone to the school in the first place only because I was handicapped, and now, as they could clearly see, I no longer needed to be there.

My parents would arrive with the car to pack up all my things and I'd walk out the front door of Second Medical — I'd be wearing jeans rolled up at the ankles, a white short-sleeved blouse, penny loafers, and white socks. I'd walk across the lawn, swinging my arms, striding without a limp, no crutches, no braces, no lift necessary on my penny loafers in spite of the three-inch difference in my legs.

My friends would be amazed.

I was in bed in the Girls' Ward, dressed, sitting against a pillow, my Survival Notebook in my lap, a letter from Harold Ickes, saying he'd gotten word I would be heading home in May, lying open on the bed.

It was a Friday morning, the first week of April, and I was waiting for my father.

The ward was oddly quiet after breakfast, the beds full except for that of Avie Crider, who had gone home. In the next bed, Sandy Newcombe peered over her Hardy Boys to watch me, and I pretended not to notice. No one spoke, but I understood that and was just as glad to sit in silence. The girls didn't know what to say to me, so they busied themselves with drawing or reading or writing or playing solitaire on their laps, avoiding conversation.

I had asked Miss Riley if I could get dressed and wait for my father downstairs in the waiting room, and she said I needed to stay in the ward.

I didn't have the heart to read or write, and just the effort of following my thoughts to some kind of dead end was exhausting, and so I simply sat there, a lead weight, looking beyond Sandy's bed out the window, which overlooked the woods, dappled with sunlight.

I had rehearsed my last day at Warm Springs many times. I'd go back to the Girls' Ward with my parents after they had arrived — it would be sunny and warm and breezy because we were in the mountains. I'd stand at the door and call *goodbye* and *thank you. Thank you for everything, my good friends for life. Thank you for this year,* I'd say. And everyone, bed to bed, all of my new friends and old ones, even Caroline Slover, still in a semiprivate room, would cry a symphony of tears at my departure. I'd walk down the corridor past Magnolia, waving at me from under the table, her big eyes red as apples, and stop at the Babies' Ward, kiss Paisley Jean, who would be weeping, and blow kisses to all my babies, *Goodbye, goodbye, my darling babies, my darling ones.* Joey would be at the front door with a silver bracelet he had had engraved — *To Suzie. I love you. Joey.* But I had to leave, had to go home to my regular life, so I'd kiss Joey on the cheek and tell him we'd write each other every day.

I'd walk out the front door between my proud parents, waving and waving to the windows behind me, waving to the world ahead.

Father James had come up to the Girls' Ward the night before, after lights out, and sat down on the side of my bed.

"I have to tell you before you hear it from someone else that Cynthia died yesterday morning."

I didn't cry. Not then and not for weeks after I had left Warm Springs. Not until I'd gone home, when I tried to fall asleep, with Rosie's little face on the inside of my eyelids.

"She had a strep infection and it just . . ." He lifted his arms in the air in a gesture of hopelessness.

"I called her Rosie," I said. "That was my name for her."

So Father James had been called to the Children's Ward for last rites the morning of the day Joey and I had raced down the hill.

Would it have made a difference if Father James had told me about Rosie before I had met Joey for the race? Would I have been deterred?

Occasionally I have wanted to die, and that was one of the times. I remember it clearly.

"Do you want to talk to me?" Father James asked.

He knew better than to mention Joey.

I shook my head.

When I reread *Wooden and Wicker* at the beginning of my research for this book, I was pleased to find in that quite awful manuscript so much valuable information, factual and personal, about Warm Springs. I needed it to jar my memory. When, at the end of the book, the young boy and the girl protagonist, slimly disguised as Victoria, are stopped in their wheelchairs at the top of the sharp incline between the buildings at Warm Springs, I felt a nervous anticipation, as if I were reading the story for the first time.

The girl and boy start down the hill, going faster and faster. Speeding dangerously and nearing the bottom, their grip tight on the wheels, they spin out of control and fly out of their chairs into the air.

And then something surprising happens in the book.

In this imagined version of my young girl's reality, the race ends in a terrible accident: the boy is bruised but otherwise unharmed, and the girl is nearly fatally injured.

I was stunned. I had no idea until then that I had rewritten the real end of the story so that it came out *right* — that I, though the perpetrator in the book, am also the victim. All those years between the writing of that book and the reading of it, I had believed that, in my novel, I'd told the truth.

Miss Riley had come to my room early on the morning after the accident.

"We have called your parents," she said. "Your father will be here by this afternoon and will take you home."

"But this is my home until I'm well enough to leave," I said. "I'm not well yet."

"You're well enough to go home," Miss Riley said.

"I was told by Dr. Iler," I said, gathering my wits about me, "that no one left Warm Springs until she was as well as possible. And I'm not that well. I can hardly walk and I'm in very much pain."

"You'll be fine," she said. "Not to worry."

My father was wearing a suit, the Washington morning paper folded under his arm, an empty suitcase in his other hand. Miss Riley was with him, leading the way. The girls looked up, then down to their business, as Miss Riley pulled the curtain around my bed.

"I don't believe she has very much to pack," she said, and left us there alone.

He wasn't angry. He wasn't anything at all, simply a father who had come to pick up his daughter, dismissed in disgrace. He packed my clothes, something I'd never seen him do, folding them hastily.

"Is that all?" he asked.

I put in the books my mother had sent, my Survival Notebook, my packet of letters, and he closed the suitcase.

"Ready?" he asked.

"I can't walk," I said. "You heard that."

I put on my brace and my orthopedic shoe with the high lift and picked up the crutches that were leaning against the night table.

An orderly came in with a wheelchair and I sat in it.

"Someone from Warm Springs is driving us to the Atlanta airport," my father said.

I put the crutches across the arms of the wheelchair and headed out in front of my father.

I hadn't considered how to leave after the circumstances of my departure changed.

I stopped at the door, my father beside me.

"Goodbye," I called, hoping that my voice sounded strong. "It's been really fun."

"Goodbye." "Goodbye." "Goodbye." "Goodbye."

"It's been really, really fun," Sandy Newcombe called after me, and her voice was breaking. I *think* I heard that her voice was breaking.

As I turned to go through the door of the Girls' Ward for the last time, Sandy — I should have expected this, I should have known it would happen, that Sandy would be the one — started singing, and then they all joined in:

> Put another muscle in
> Where the quadriceps have been
> 'Cause we know we'll never win
> With traces, traces, traces.

> What's the use of stretch and strain
> What's the good of pull and pain
> When our muscle tests remain
> Just traces, traces, traces.

They push our torso
And make it more so
When we try to make a muscle go
It's substitution, no, no, no.

So even though our hopes have soared
Higher than our muscles scored
Just the same we thank the Lord
For traces, traces, traces.

I could hear the words all the way down the corridor, past the nurses' station where Miss Riley was standing, and to my astonishment she leaned over, put a bony hand on my shoulder, and kissed my cheek.

My father pressed the down button and pushed me into the elevator.

Paisley Jean was standing at the door of the Children's Ward as I wheeled past, and I couldn't look, not at her, not through the door at the babies. I was afraid I would cry and never stop crying.

Dr. Iler walked to the car with us and shook my father's hand and handed him an envelope with the instructions for physical therapy.

"If she continues to work hard, there is no reason why she shouldn't be much better than when she arrived, but it will take time, years even."

I settled myself in the back seat, probably sitting with my arms folded defensively across my chest.

Dr. Iler leaned in the open window.

"You'll be fine, Susan Richards," he said, meeting my gaze.

My father eased into the seat next to me. He seemed more perplexed than upset. That, at least, is what I felt in the close confines of the back seat.

I hadn't asked about my mother, but he brought her up.

"Your mother doesn't fly, as you know," he said, to explain why he had been the one to come. "And they wanted you home pronto."

I hadn't spoken with my mother since the accident, but I was sure she would be more glad to have me home than upset by the reason I was coming early. I wasn't sure about anything with my father.

"I guess I sort of flunked out of Warm Springs," I said.

"That would be a fair description," he said.

"Did anyone tell you about Joey Buckley?" I asked.

"He broke his legs."

"Both legs?"

"Both."

I bit my lip until it bled salty in my mouth, but there was nothing to say, nothing to add to what was already known. Most of the trip to Atlanta we didn't talk, but sometime along the way, my father asked me what had happened.

"A lot happened," I said, but I couldn't have known the answers to his question then.

Something fundamental had taken place in those two years, some imperceptible change that had a life of its own. Character is surprising, the way it surfaces and resolves itself over and over in any life.

Once inside the plane, I asked my father why my mother was afraid to fly. It was my first time in an airplane.

"She's afraid to lose control. If something should happen, she won't know how to fly the plane."

"Do you?"

"I'm willing to leave it to the pilot," he said.

I sat in the window seat in the eighth row from the front, just over the propellers, watching the blades spin round and round and become a single blurred blade, looking out at the other planes lining up to take off.

My father reached over and fastened my seat belt.

"Now we head for the runway," he told me as I clutched the arm of the seat.

"And take off?"

"We taxi down the runway, and once we're going fast enough, we lift off the ground."

The plane was rushing forward, the roar of the propellers a high whistle in my ear.

"Is it dangerous?" I asked.

My mother had always been my barometer for danger.

"Takeoff is always riskier than landing," he said.

"Are we okay?"

"We're fine," he said. "This is normal."

I watched as the ground slipped under us, and then we were weightless, clearing the trees, angling sharply up. I caught my breath.

"Have we taken off?"

"We are in the air," he said.

Below us, the city of Atlanta spread across the landscape like a toy town glittering in the sunlight. As I settled back against the seat, the plane lurched, dipping sideways, and I felt myself tilting, off balance, my cheek against the glass as if at any moment the window would fly off and I'd be thrown into the open air, left on my own to discover the way home.

Afterword

AFTER 1954, when the Salk vaccine was introduced to the public, the polio patient population at Warm Springs began to diminish. In 1974, the state of Georgia took over the facility and created a center for stroke victims, patients with brain and spinal cord injuries and severe arthritis. Roosevelt Warm Springs is now in the process of becoming two hospitals, one medical and one vocational.

The head of surgery, Dr. Irwin, who was responsible for changing the lives of so many patients during my time there, eventually moved to Atlanta. Shortly thereafter, he suffered severe injuries in an automobile accident. Confined to a wheelchair, he failed to escape a fire in his house.

The March of Dimes has, since the success of the polio vaccine, changed its mission and now raises funds for the care of premature babies.

The hospital records from the early 1950s are now in the medical archives of the State of Georgia, where I have access only to my own file.

At the time I wrote this memoir, I did not know what had happened to Joey Buckley. And then in April 2007, shortly before the memoir was published, I had a call from Nashville, Tennessee, from a record producer who had just visited Warm Springs for the first time since he had been a patient there in 1952. So Ron Haffkine—who was the boy I've called Joey Buckley—found me. The day after we spoke, I got on a plane to Nashville and though we hadn't remembered each other's name, we knew we had been friends and have become friends once again.

ACKNOWLEDGMENTS

A NUMBER OF BOOKS about polio, the development of a rehabilitation hospital at Warm Springs, Franklin D. Roosevelt, and the National Foundation for Infantile Paralysis informed this book. In particular, the excellent *Polio: An American Story* by David Oshinsky was not only a wonderful read but also taught me a great deal I did not know. I valued Jeffrey Kluger's *Splendid Solution: Jonas Salk and the Conquest of Polio,* about the race to develop the vaccine. I discovered in *FDR's Splendid Deception* by Hugh Gregory Gallagher (himself a victim of polio, contracted in 1952) a sensitive and intuitive account of this most popular of presidents, at once outgoing and deeply private. My reading especially of Oshinsky's book shaped my understanding of the history of polio and Roosevelt's contribution to the extraordinary public health initiative that culminated in the vaccine.

I visited Warm Springs, now called Roosevelt Warm Springs, in May 2006 — the first time I returned since 1952 — and am very grateful for the history provided by Linda Creekbaum, the tour guide and Web site manager for Roosevelt Warm Springs, and to Mike Shadix, the dedicated librarian there. I spent many hours at the Franklin D. Roosevelt Presidential Library in Hyde Park reading Roosevelt's letters during his early years at Warm Springs, particularly letters to his mother and Eleanor Roosevelt, and wish to thank Alycia Vivona at the library for her considerable help.

I want to thank my editor, Deanne Urmy, on whose sensibilities and eye for detail I depend, the team at Houghton Mifflin, and my agent, Gail Hochman.

I owe much to my dear pals in life and work for all these many years: Beverly Lowry, Steve Goodwin, Alan Cheuse, and Richard Bausch. To Porter Shreve, an excellent editor. To Harold Ickes for the boy he was, loyal and true. To Alan Friedman for paying attention. To Carol Shreve for her generosity and wit. And especially to Dolores and Frank DeAngelis for their enduring friendship — always steady in the stern of any old boat our family takes out to sea.

Finally, and always, I'm grateful to my family: Timothy, Po, Bich, E. Q., Rusty, Theo, Noah, Caleb, Jess, and Kate.